D1174966

NASA AERONAUTICS BOOK SERIES

A New Twist in Flight Research

The F-18 Active
Aeroelastic
Wing Project

Peter W. Merlin

Library of Congress Cataloging-in-Publication Data

Merlin, Peter W., 1964-
  A new twist in flight research : the F-18 active aeroelastic wing project / by
Peter W. Merlin.
       pages cm
  Includes bibliographical references and index.
1. Hornet (Jet fighter plane)--Design and construction. I. Title. II. Title:
F-18 active aeroelastic wing project.
  UG1242.F5.M474 2013
  629.134'32--dc23
                                        2013032588

ISBN 978-1-62683-012-7

9 781626 830127

This publication is available as a free download at
http://www.nasa.gov/ebooks.

Table of Contents

Wilbur Wright makes a right turn in the 1902 glider. The three-axis control system made this craft the world's first fully controllable flying machine. (Library of Congress)

INTRODUCTION:
The Wright Way to Fly

The human desire to fly can be traced back at least as far as the second century B.C. Greek legend of Icarus, who attempted to fly with wings made from bird feathers and beeswax. Since birds are naturally efficient flyers, it is not surprising that they have served as an inspiration to both casual observers and serious scholars of flight.[1] In fact, lessons learned from the study of birds in centuries past may have a significant impact on future aircraft development. National Aeronautics and Space Administration (NASA), Air Force, and industry researchers are using wing-shaping techniques that emulate the flexibility of bird wings to develop flight controls for 21st-century airplanes.[2]

Florentine painter, sculptor, and scientist Leonardo da Vinci (1452–1519) undertook some of the most serious early study of avian flying characteristics. His extensive scientific observations led him to focus on how birds controlled their flight by changing the shape of their wings to take advantage of wind and air currents. He also made anatomical studies of bird and bat wings to define their structural characteristics. Eventually, da Vinci designed a glider capable of supporting the weight of a man. Bat-like wings featured a fixed inner section and a mobile outer section that could be flexed by hand-controlled cables. The flier's position, with the wings balanced upon his shoulders, allowed him to maintain balance by moving the lower part of his body. A tail assembly provided additional stability.[3]

These concepts saw their first practical application four centuries later in the designs of Wilbur and Orville Wright, of Dayton, OH, brothers who lacked formal training in engineering or science. Their interest in solving the

---

1. Richard P. Hallion, *Test Pilots: The Frontiersmen of Flight* (Washington, DC: Smithsonian Institution Press, 1988), p. 1.
2. Ed Pendleton, "Back to the Future: How Active Aeroelastic Wings are a Return to Aviation's Beginnings and a Small Step to Future Bird-Like Wings," presented at the RTO AVT Symposium on Active Control Technology for Enhanced Performance Operational Capabilities of Military Aircraft, Land Vehicles and Sea Vehicles, Braunschweig, Germany, May 2000.
3. Martin Kemp, *Leonardo da Vinci, the Marvellous Works of Nature and Man* (Cambridge, MA: Harvard University Press, 1981), pp. 104–106, 248–250.

problems of flight, however, was driven by a methodical, scientific engineering approach. Most important, they intuitively understood that control and stability were the most crucial problems in aeronautics, and they set about solving those problems through incremental flying experiments. As with numerous predecessors, the Wrights began by studying birds.

The issue of lateral stability and control—roll motion—was especially challenging. After reading about the mechanics of bird flight, they observed buzzards circling and determined that birds controlled their rate of roll by tilting one wingtip up and the other down simultaneously. The brothers then sought to apply their observations to an experimental biplane box kite. Wilbur Wright inadvertently stumbled on the solution in the early summer of 1899 while idly twisting a small cardboard box between his thumbs and index fingers. Envisioning the upper and lower surfaces of the box as the airfoils of a kite, he conceived steering a biplane system by twisting the airfoils—a principle that came to be known as wing warping.[4]

Leonardo da Vinci sketched birds in flight and made landmark discoveries about center of gravity and air currents by observing how birds stay aloft without flapping their wings. His studies, detailed in the *Codex on the Flight of Birds* (ca. 1490–1505), inspired several designs for flying machines. (Author's collection)

The Wrights immediately tested their new concept using a box kite with a 5-foot span. Using cables to twist the airfoils, they quickly determined that they were on the right track to solve the problem of lateral control. Confidence gained through such rudimentary flight-testing paved the way for piloted trials using a full-scale glider. In 1900, the brothers built a biplane kite-glider with a 17-foot wingspan and a forward-mounted horizontal elevator (dubbed a "front rudder") and shipped it to Kitty Hawk, NC. The windswept dunes of Kitty Hawk provided an ideal location for flight experiments. During initial trials, the craft was flown as a kite, but the brothers also conducted a few piloted flights as well, before returning to Dayton.

In the summer of 1901, they tested a second glider at a site in Kill Devil Hills, four miles south of Kitty Hawk. The results were disappointing, as the craft had an alarming tendency to sideslip uncontrollably toward the ground

---

4. Hallion, *Test Pilots*, pp. 26–27.

HOW THE WINGS WERE WARPED

RIGHT   LEFT

CRADLE

→ → → CABLES ATTACHED TO CRADLE — SLIDING CRADLE TO LEFT
OF MACHINE PULLS TRAILING EDGE OF RIGHT WING DOWNWARD

→————→ CABLE (NOT ATTACHED TO CRADLE) IS MOVED
AUTOMATICALLY BY DOWNWARD MOVEMENT OF RIGHT WING

The Wrights developed a method for controlling their aircraft by twisting the airfoils. This wing-warping technique became a standard feature of their early airplanes. (Al Bowers collection)

during wing warping. In evident frustration, Wilbur exclaimed, "Nobody will fly for a thousand years!"[5]

The Wrights went back to the drawing board, tenaciously working to develop more reliable aerodynamic data. They also tested more than 200 airfoil shapes in a wind tunnel. The end result was a new craft that, like its predecessors, featured a spruce frame supporting a muslin fabric covering. The biplane had longer, narrower wings spanning 32 feet, and a thinner airfoil. Design features included a canard elevator for pitch control, wing warping for lateral control, and a fixed dual-surface vertical rudder to improve stability in turns. The wings were drooped downward slightly to counteract sideslip due to crosswinds.

During flight-testing, the Wrights discovered that unequal drag produced by wing warping gave the 1902 glider a tendency to develop adverse yaw that could not be countered using the fixed rudder. They resolved the problem by linking a moveable rudder to the wing-warping mechanism, which was controlled by a hip cradle. When the prone pilot moved the cradle—reminiscent of Leonardo da Vinci's glider steering mechanism—the wings twisted, and the rudder automatically assumed the necessary position for the desired turn. This three-axis control system made the Wrights' 1902 glider the world's first fully controllable aircraft.[6]

After gaining additional flying experience through hundreds of glide flights, the brothers began construction of the 1903 Wright Flyer, their first powered aircraft. It was a biplane with a 40-foot span, driven by a 12-horsepower petroleum-fueled engine that drove two pusher propellers. The first flight on December 17, 1903, lasted only 12 seconds and ended just 120 feet from its starting point. The brothers took turns, completing four flights that day, the longest lasting 59

5. Ibid., p. 28.
6. Ibid., p. 28.

The first flight of the Wright's powered flyer took place on December 17, 1903. The distance traveled was equivalent to the fuselage length of a modern commercial transport. (Library of Congress)

seconds and covering a distance of 852 feet. Following this historic milestone, the Wrights returned to Dayton to develop improved airplane designs that could be flown repeatedly and reliably. Although they continued to use the wing warping technique until 1911, they began experimenting in 1905 with a three-control system that would dominate aircraft controls throughout the 20th century.[7]

Despite the Wright's innovative use of flexible airfoils, wing flexibility affected other early airplane designs adversely. In fact, this characteristic likely thwarted Samuel Pierpont Langley's attempt to develop a powered aircraft in 1903. Langley, secretary of the Smithsonian Institution, designed a tandem monoplane with a 48-foot span and a distinct dihedral (up sweep). It was driven by a 52.4-horsepower engine and launched by catapult from atop a houseboat on the Potomac River. Langley's assistant, Charles Manly, made two attempts to fly the craft in October and December 1903, but each ended in dismal failure as the flying machine pitched down into the icy waters. The first mishap resulted from a malfunction of the launch mechanism, in which a pin failed to release and snagged a bracing wire on the front of the wing.[8] On

7. Ibid., pp. 29–31.

8. Ibid., pp. 23–26.

the second attempt, the wings snapped due to excessive flight loads, possibly resulting from torsional divergence.[9]

Over the next several decades, designers worked to produce airplanes capable of withstanding higher speeds and greater aerodynamic loads. This resulted in configurations with semi-monocoque structures in which the loads are carried partly by the frame and stringers, and partly by the skin. While flying these aircraft, pilots soon discovered a wide variety of aeroelastic problems including, among others, wing flutter, divergence, buffeting, and control reversal. Designers responded by increasing wing stiffness, but this also increased structural weight. Aircraft designers often opted to reduce wingspan, increase airfoil thickness, and accept reduced aerodynamic performance in exchange for increased speed.[10]

In the early part of the 21st century, advances in materials and adaptive control technologies allowed aeronautical researchers to revisit the wing-warping control technique pioneered by the Wright brothers and to take a small step toward development of wings with a bird-like capability for changing shape to optimize efficiency. This new concept, now known as Active Aeroelastic Wing (AAW), is a synergistic technology that integrates air vehicle aerodynamics, active controls, and structures to maximize aircraft performance. The concept turns aeroelastic flexibility—once a liability—into a net benefit through the use of multiple leading- and trailing-edge control surfaces activated by a digital flight control system. Using these surfaces to control the wing's aeroelastic twist allows energy from the airstream to provide desired roll forces. When the aircraft is subject to high dynamic pressures, the AAW control surfaces may be used in the same manner that aerodynamic tabs are used to apply a force moment that causes the control surfaces to change incidence and achieve trim. In the case of AAW, the control surface acts as the tab and the resulting moment counters an adverse aeroelastic twist. Additionally, AAW controls can minimize drag at low wing-strain conditions and/or minimize structural loads at high wing-strain conditions. With AAW technology, a lightweight flexible wing now has a positive effect for generating control power rather than a negative one.[11]

AAW technology is considered especially synergistic with the use of thin, flexible wings, allowing designers more freedom to exploit efficient, high-aspect-ratio airfoils. Such technology may be used to improve the capabilities of existing wing planforms as well as to reduce conflicting requirements between stiff versus flexible wings for new aircraft with multiple mission requirements.

---

9. Pendleton, "Back to the Future."

10. Ibid.

11. Ibid.

Potential benefits resulting from the application of AAW technology to future aircraft include increased control power from conventional control surfaces by maintaining their effectiveness, optimized control-surface deflections to reduce aerodynamic drag, improved lifting efficiency, and reduced aircraft structural weight.[12]

In the first step toward these goals, a joint effort by NASA, Air Force, and Boeing researchers resulted in an AAW test bed that eventually came to be known as the X-53. The experiment used a modified F-18 Hornet[13] (a Navy fighter plane) equipped with more flexible wing panels from a preproduction prototype, independently operated inboard and outboard leading- and trailing-edge flaps, and advanced flight control computers. Flight control software included new AAW control laws that actively commanded optimal trim settings to facilitate aeroelastic wing twist and minimize loads at high speeds.[14]

Essential elements of AAW technology include exploitation of aeroelastic flexibility to maximize control power and optimization of control laws to reduce structural loads and drag. The AAW flight research program at NASA Dryden Flight Research Center, in Edwards, CA, began in 1996 with completion of wing modifications and extensive instrumentation for data collection. Reassembly was completed by early 2001, and over the course of the year, control software was installed in the research flight computer, and the airplane was subjected to extensive structural loads, wing stiffness and vibration tests, systems checkout, and flight simulation.[15]

The flight-test program was divided into two phases. The first, beginning in late 2002, consisted of research flights for parameter identification to measure the forces available from the leading-edge and trailing-edge control surfaces to twist the wing and control the aircraft. In April 2003, researchers began a 12-month period of data analysis and control software redesign to optimize AAW wing performance. The second phase of flight tests, from late 2004 to March 2005, allowed researchers to evaluate AAW control laws as well as the airplane's performance and handling qualities. Two research pilots collected data at 18 test points ranging from speeds of Mach 0.85 to Mach 1.3 and altitudes ranging from 5,000 to 25,000 feet. Several additional flights were flown

---

12. Scott Zillmer, "Integrated Maneuver Load Control (MLC) for Active Flexible Wing (AFW) Design—Final Briefing," Boeing North American Aircraft Division, May 21, 1997, from personal files of Ed Pendleton.

13. The Hornet debuted as the F-18 in 1978 but was redesignated F/A-18 in 1980 to highlight its expanded role as an attack aircraft. Since NASA routinely uses the original designation for the Agency's aircraft, the author has done so as well for the sake of clarity.

14. Pendleton, "Back to the Future."

15. Ibid.

A modified F-18 jet fighter served as a test bed for AAW technology. The joint Air Force–NASA-Boeing effort demonstrated a modern equivalent of the wing-warping concept. (NASA)

to re-evaluate several test points with modified control laws and to evaluate the ability of the AAW system to alleviate wing structural loads.[16]

Data from the flight research program effectively demonstrated the AAW concept at comparatively low cost. The AAW project received funding from NASA's Aeronautics Research Mission Directorate, as well as from the U.S. Air Force Research Laboratory (AFRL). The Boeing Company's Phantom Works division in St. Louis, MO, performed the necessary wing modifications, installed instrumentation, and assisted in software development under contract with the AFRL and NASA. The program's total budget of approximately $45 million included about $29 million in direct monetary outlay and $16 million for in-kind support, spread over 8 years.[17]

The successful demonstration of actively controlled wing-warping techniques for aircraft roll control at transonic speeds provided benchmark design criteria as guidance for future aircraft designs. Aeronautical engineers can use the results in designing more efficient, thinner, higher-aspect-ratio wings for future high-performance aircraft while reducing structural weight of the wings by approximately 10 to 20 percent. Resulting benefits will include increased fuel efficiency, payload capability, and potentially reduced radar signature. AAW technology has applications to future fighters, transports, and airliners, as well as to high-altitude/long-endurance remotely piloted aircraft.[18]

---

16. NASA Fact Sheet, "Back to the Future: Active Aeroelastic Wing Flight Research," *http://www.nasa.gov/centers/dryden/news/FactSheets/FS-061-DFRC.html*, December 9, 2009 (accessed May 15, 2012).

17. Ibid.

18. Ibid.

This multiple-exposure image shows the AFW model at various angles of attack in the NASA Langley Transonic Dynamics Tunnel. (NASA)

CHAPTER 1:

Origins and Design Development

Aeronautical researchers have studied aeroelastic phenomena (the interaction between inertial, elastic, and aerodynamic forces on aircraft structures) since the 1920s in order to solve problems associated with static aeroelasticity, flutter, and dynamic loads. Efforts in the 1940s and 1950s (continuing into the 1980s) focused on flutter suppression and development of accurate prediction methods. Additional studies identified flutter parameters to be used in a database for aeroelastic design and analysis. Characteristics of unsteady aerodynamics and development of aero-elastic prediction methods for flight in the transonic, supersonic, and hypersonic regimes were key research areas during the 1960s. Throughout the 1970s, Air Force and industry researchers made major improvements in linear unsteady aero-dynamic prediction tools for computing transonic flow forces around oscillating airfoils and planar wings. Wind tunnel testing validated various prediction meth-ods, which soon became international standards for validation of emerging compu-tational prediction methods. In 1975, the Air Force Flight Dynamics Laboratory (AFFDL), at Wright-Patterson Air Force Base, OH, contracted Grumman Aircraft Corporation to develop a computer program for iterative, converging flutter and strength design of metallic aircraft structures. By 1978, a modified version of the program extended the method to include composite structures that were quickly becoming commonplace on modern airplanes.[1]

With AFFDL sponsorship, General Dynamics Corporation developed a tai-loring and structural optimization (TSO) method that aircraft designers could use to control static and dynamic aeroelastic deformation to improve aerody-namic and structural performance. After spearheading numerous improve-ments to the TSO technique, AFFDL researchers assisted with the design of the Highly Maneuverable Aircraft Technology (HiMAT) demonstrator, a remotely piloted research vehicle. The HiMAT, built by Rockwell International for a joint Air Force–NASA research program, was the first airplane to fly with aeroelastically tailored lifting surfaces.[2]

---

1. Terry M. Harris and Lawrence J. Huttsell, "Aeroelasticity Research at Wright-Patterson Air Force Base (Wright Field) from 1953–1993," *Journal of Aircraft* 40, no. 5 (September–October 2003), pp. 813–819.

2. Ibid.

AFW Wind Tunnel Model Testing

In the early 1980s, the AFFDL embarked on research into control system/aeroelastic interactions. The first major test effort, known as the Active Flexible Wing (AFW), was developed based on a Rockwell concept that employed multiple control surfaces to take advantage of the airstream's power to shape the wing for improved roll rates or efficient cruise. The results of several contracted investigations and tests of a transonic wind tunnel model indicated that use of such technology could also substantially reduce aircraft takeoff weight.[3]

The AFW concept exploits wing flexibility to reduce weight and improve aerodynamics. Proper control of aeroelastic twist can result in improved maneuver aerodynamics at several subsonic, transonic, and supersonic design points. Active flexible wings manufactured from lightweight alloys and composite materials would be designed to withstand critical air and ground loads, and they would have sufficient stiffness to prevent buckling or flutter within the design performance envelope. Additional weight reduction is realized through elimination of conventional horizontal tail surfaces. Roll can be controlled through the use of multiple leading- and trailing-edge control surfaces on the wings. In a conventional aircraft design, too much wing twist leads to aileron reversal over a significant portion of the flight envelope, degrading roll performance. Aileron reversal occurs when the aileron's contribution to roll control is reversed due to overall wing flexibility. Aircraft designers often correct this problem by stiffening the wing or through the use of a tail with a differential capability that can be used to roll the aircraft. With the AFW concept, an active roll control system manages roll performance solely through combinations of leading- and trailing-edge flaps. The elimination of additional wing stiffness—normally added to preclude aileron reversal—would probably mean that on a high-aspect-ratio wing, outboard ailerons would likely be susceptible to reversal at high dynamic pressures. Active control systems for flutter suppression, gust load alleviation, and maneuver load alleviation offer further opportunities for weight reduction.[4]

Engineers from Rockwell's North American Aircraft Division, in Los Angeles, CA, applied this technology while performing design studies to develop a proposal for the Advanced Tactical Fighter (ATF) design competition that eventually spawned the F-22 Raptor. These studies in 1983 and 1984, which included low-speed wind tunnel testing, suggested that AFW technology

---

3. Ibid.
4. Boyd Perry III, Stanley R. Cole, and Gerald D. Miller, "Summary of an Active Flexible Wing Program," *Journal of Aircraft* 32, no. 1 (January–February 1995), p. 10.

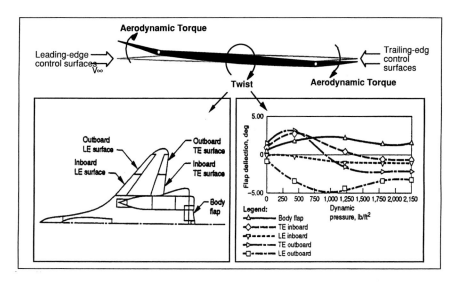

Rockwell's AFW concept exploited aerodynamic torque to control rolling motion. (NASA)

could reduce the takeoff gross weight of the ATF by approximately 18 percent. Transonic model testing began in 1985 using the Transonic Dynamics Tunnel (TDT) at NASA's Langley Flight Research Center, in Hampton, VA, under a contract from the Air Force Wright Aeronautical Laboratory (AFWAL).[5]

Under this contract, the AFWAL paid Rockwell to conduct tests in the TDT, which was provided by Langley through an agreement with the Air Force. Using company funds, Rockwell built a full-span, aeroelastically scaled AFW test bed model representing an advanced tactical fighter configuration with two leading-edge and two trailing-edge control surfaces driven by electrohydraulic actuators. The sting-mounted model was attached to allow it freedom to roll about the axis of the sting or be locked in place for static testing.[6]

Two independent AFW study programs utilized the AFW wind tunnel test bed model. The first, sponsored by the Air Force, NASA, and Rockwell, focused on demonstrating the basic AFW concept during two tests in 1986 and 1987. The first program proved the AFW concept in the wind tunnel. The

5. Notes on "Active Aeroelastic Wing (AAW) Technology Previous Efforts/Opportunities," March 1996, provided by Dave Voracek, NASA Dryden Flight Research Center, from personal files.

6. Stanley R. Cole, Thomas E. Noll, and Boyd Perry III, "Transonic Dynamics Tunnel Aeroelastic Testing in Support of Aircraft Development," *Journal of Aircraft* 40, no. 5 (September–October 2003), p. 826.

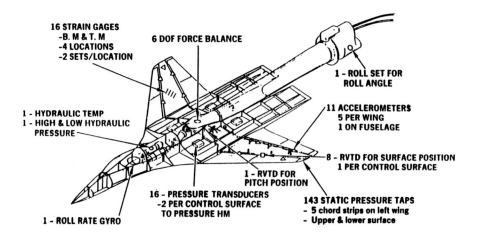

The AFW wind tunnel model had six degrees of freedom and was extensively instrumented. (NASA)

second, encompassing two test entries sponsored by NASA and Rockwell in 1989 and 1991, demonstrated digital active controls technology in combination with AFW.[7]

Researchers installed the AFW model in Langley's TDT, a closed-circuit, continuous-flow wind tunnel capable of speeds from zero to Mach 1.2 and static stagnation pressures ranging from near zero to atmospheric. The test section, which could be pressurized with air or a heavy gas test medium, had a 15-foot-square cross section with cropped corners. Testing in 1986–1987 was done using a heavy gas medium; air was used in later tests. The TDT was equipped with four quick-actuating bypass valves connecting the test section to the opposite leg of the tunnel circuit downstream of the drive fan motor. In the event of model instability, such as flutter, instrumentation automatically commanded the valves to open in order to reduce Mach number and dynamic pressure.[8]

The AFW wind tunnel model represented a notional advanced fighter aircraft configuration with a blended wing-body configuration. The full-span, aeroelastically scaled model had low-aspect-ratio swept wings and twin outwardly canted vertical stabilizers spaced apart on either side of the exhaust deck. Each wing was equipped with two leading-edge and two trailing-edge control surfaces driven by electrohydraulic actuators.[9] These surfaces were restricted

---

7. Perry, Cole, and Miller, "Summary of an Active Flexible Wing Program."

8. Ibid.

9. Cole, Noll, and Perry, "Transonic Dynamics Tunnel Aeroelastic Testing in Support of Aircraft Development."

to ±10 degrees deflection to avoid hinge-moment and wing-load limitations. The model was sting mounted in the TDT on a mechanism that allowed the model to roll about the sting if required. A pivot arrangement made it possible to adjust the model's pitch angle from approximately −1.5 degrees to 13.5 degrees.[10]

The two wind tunnel test entries in 1986 and 1987 were essential for proving the AFW concept. The aircraft model, aerodynamics, structures, and controls characterization demonstrated in the first entry and the AFW control law and maneuver load control laws verified in the second allowed AFWAL researchers to move forward with additional application studies and, subsequently, a full-scale flight research program. Wind tunnel results, along with conceptual design studies conducted by Rockwell prior to the contracted effort, verified that the AFW concept was feasible for full-scale application and would provide improved aircraft performance. The model's wing structure was relatively flexible but satisfied strength and flutter design requirements. Maximum control-surface deflections never exceeded 5 degrees, as compared with the 30- to 40-degree trailing-edge control-surface deflections necessary to maintain the same roll rate with a stiffer conventional wing design. These smaller deflections resulted in reduced drag and reduced surface hinge moments. Researchers estimated the benefits of AFW technology in terms of takeoff gross weight (TOGW) by examining changes in structural and system weight along with improvements in aerodynamic performance. They estimated a 15- to 30-percent reduction in TOGW for a constant performing aircraft.[11]

Additional Areas of Study

AFW researchers also pursued studies of active flutter suppression, a separate but related technology with the potential to prevent catastrophic actuator failure on a full-scale AFW aircraft. Prior to the November 1989 test, technicians fitted the model with wingtip ballast stores for an active flutter suppression (AFS) demonstration. Each store consisted of a thin, hollow aluminum tube containing internal ballast to lower the wing's flutter boundary to a desired dynamic pressure range. This modification also lowered the model's flutter speed to within the operating envelope of the TDT. A pitch-pivot mechanism for attaching the ballast store to the wingtip allowed the pod to pitch relative to

---

10. Perry, Cole, and Miller, "Summary of an Active Flexible Wing Program."

11. Gerald D. Miller, "Active Flexible Wing (AFW) Technology," Air Force Wright Aeronautical Laboratories, TR-87-3096 (February 1988).

the airfoil surface. The pivot could be locked, or coupled, to the wingtip during flutter testing, and instantly unlocked in the event of flutter instability. In the decoupled configuration, reduced stiffness increased the frequency of the wing's first torsion mode, moving the flutter condition to higher dynamic pressures. Compatibility of AFW with systems for AFS, rolling maneuver load alleviation (RMLA), and roll-rate tracking was crucial to demonstrating multiple-input, multiple-output (MIMO) multiple-function digital control laws.[12]

The TDT tests also provided practical experience in designing, fabricating, and implementing a real-time MIMO multiple-function digital controller for use with the wind tunnel model. For increased fidelity, the model controller needed to accurately represent the version to be used on a full-scale airplane. It had to be programmed with easily modified or replaceable control laws and be capable of sending and receiving both analog and discrete signals. It was necessary for the controller to be capable of recording, storing, and transfer-ring digitized signals. It also had to be capable of simultaneous execution of both flutter suppression and rolling maneuver control laws, and it had to allow for manual positioning of flight control surfaces. A SUN 3/160 workstation driven by a Unix operating system served as a shell for the controller. Hardware components included a host computer, two digital signal processors boards, analog-to-digital and digital-to-analog conversion boards, and an array pro-cessor board. Primary and backup systems afforded redundancy in case of a processor board failure. Programmers developed a generic form of the control law structure that allowed for changes to be easily and reliably implemented.[13]

In preparation for wind tunnel testing, researchers at NASA Langley devel-oped aeroelastic equations of motion for the AFW model. These equations rep-resented numerous combinations of Mach number and dynamic pressure for four model configurations including fixed-in-roll (coupled and uncoupled) and free-to-roll (coupled and uncoupled). Programmers at Langley used Rockwell's finite-element structural model of the AFW test article as a starting point on which to build a database of mode shapes, frequencies, and generalized masses for symmetric and antisymmetric elastic modes. Data for all model configu-rations included control-surface deflection modes, but only the free-to-roll configurations featured rigid-body roll modes.[14]

The Langley team created linear aeroelastic equations of motion, combining aerodynamic forces with stiffness, damping, and mass matrices. These second-order, reduced-frequency-dependent equations were then used to perform flutter

---

12. Perry, Cole, and Miller, "Summary of an Active Flexible Wing Program."

13. Ibid.

14. Ibid.

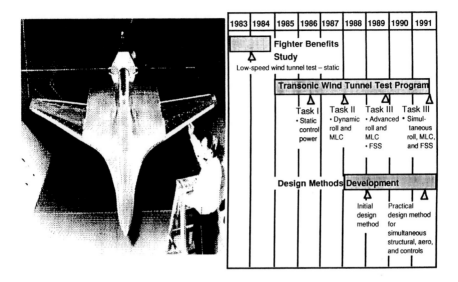

1983	1984	1985	1986	1987	1988	1989	1990	1991

Fighter Benefits Study

Low-speed wind tunnel test – static

Transonic Wind Tunnel Test Program

Task I	Task II	Task III	Task III
• Static control power	• Dynamic roll and MLC	• Advanced roll and MLC • FSS	• Simul-taneous roll, MLC, and FSS

Design Methods Development

Initial design method

Practical design method for simultaneous structural, aero, and controls

AFW analytical studies and wind tunnel testing spanned nearly a decade and provided valuable data for developing the Active Aeroelastic Wing concept. (NASA)

calculations. Application of rational function approximations to the generalized aerodynamic forces allowed researchers to develop first-order linear-time-invariant state-space equations for use in designing control laws for the AFW model.[15]

Two nonlinear simulations—a batch simulation and a hot-bench simulation—supported preparations for the 1989 and 1991 wind tunnel tests. First, control law designers used the nonlinear batch simulation as a "truth model" to evaluate control laws in terms of predicted performance and to establish gain and phase margins. Using Langley's Interaction of Structures, Aerodynamics, and Controls (ISAC) program, they combined corrected linear equations of motion with refinements to include asymmetries and nonlinearities. This allowed the aeroelastic equations of motion to be rewritten as whole-aircraft equations, which permitted individual modeling of both right- and left-side actuators and incorporation of actuator rate limits as functions of load. The batch simulation also modeled the characteristics of electronic equipment including delays associated with the digital controller.[16]

The hot-bench simulation verified the controller's functionality and made it possible to identify software errors, hardware malfunctions, and system faults. The hot-bench simulation was made with Langley's Advanced Real-Time

---

15. Ibid.

16. Ibid.

Simulation (ARTS) system, consisting of two Control Data Corporation Cyber 175 computers connected by a 50-megabit-per-second fiber-optic digital data network to an array of simulation sites. The hot-bench simulation provided human operators of the digital controller with valuable practice. More important, end-to-end verification and debugging of the complex, one-of-a-kind controller mechanism reduced risk to both the model and the wind tunnel facility during flutter testing.[17]

Control Law Development and Test Results

Four teams at Langley worked on the design of flutter suppression system (FSS) control laws for the AFW model, while two other teams developed rolling maneuver control laws. Design goals included increasing the lowest open-loop flutter dynamic pressure by 30 percent, the wind tunnel limit. Researchers discovered that, for the fixed-in-roll model configuration, both symmetric and antisymmetric flutter modes had to be suppressed in order to demonstrate even a modest increase in dynamic pressure. The free-to-roll configuration required only a symmetric FSS.[18]

The rolling maneuver control laws were designed to reduce or limit wing loads during rolls up to 90 degrees of bank. Control law designers had to ensure stability, acceptable control-surface activity, and constant roll performance in the free-to-roll configuration. An RMLA system employed gain feedback and low-pass filters, using the roll rate gyro as the primary sensor, and two pairs of control surfaces. A roll rate tracking system (RRTS) included lookup tables that contained values of control-surface deflection as functions of measured roll rate and of the difference between measured and commanded roll rates. The RRTS, which used three pairs of control surfaces and used the rate gyro as the sensor, limited loads only when they reached a predetermined level.[19]

Testing of the AFW wind tunnel model in 1989 and 1991 provided research teams with control law validation, digital controller performance evaluation, plant estimation, and root-mean-square (RMS) calculations. Experiments included single-function and multiple-function testing to explore flutter modes and rolling maneuver performance. Validation of flutter-suppression control laws and assessment of model safety risks were conducted through open-loop

---

17. Carey S. Buttrill and Jacob A. Houck, "Hot-Bench Simulation of the Active Flexible Wing Wind-Tunnel Model," Langley Research Center, NASA TM-102758 (November 1990).

18. Perry, Cole, and Miller, "Summary of an Active Flexible Wing Program."

19. Ibid.

testing that determined flutter boundaries. Each of four flutter-suppression control laws was successfully tested in the free-to-roll configuration. All four suppressed flutter to a dynamic pressure condition 23 percent beyond symmetric flutter dynamic pressure. Although this did not represent the closed-loop flutter boundary, testing to higher dynamic pressures was not possible due to TDT operating limitations. Three of the four flutter-suppression control laws were successfully demonstrated in the fixed-in-roll configuration; the fourth was not tested. During each test run, the control laws effectively suppressed both symmetric and antisymmetric flutter modes simultaneously at conditions up to 26 percent beyond antisymmetric and up to 17 percent beyond symmetric-open-loop flutter dynamic pressures. Maximum test conditions were limited due to the high dynamic response of the model's wing surfaces for all flutter-suppression control laws demonstrated.[20]

Researchers accomplished both single-function and multiple-function active controls testing. For the single-function tests, the Langley team independently validated two RMLA control laws and one RRTS control law during the 1991 test. In the coupled configuration, the RMLA and RRTS control laws were tested below the open-loop symmetric flutter condition. In the decoupled configuration, the RMLA control laws were tested to a dynamic pressure of 250 pounds per square foot (psf) while the RRTS control law was tested at 250 psf and 290 psf. A comparison of analytical and wind tunnel results revealed that the RRTS limited torsion moments to below 1,400 inch-pounds in the analytical model and to below 1,800 inch-pounds in the TDT.[21]

MIMO multiple-function control laws were demonstrated with the AFW model in simulated cruise and in rolling maneuvers. In cruise mode, all four combinations of flutter suppression and rolling maneuver control laws were validated up to the maximum dynamic pressure conditions attainable in the TDT (290 psf). In the rolling mode, flutter suppression and rolling maneuver control laws were operated simultaneously during maneuvers above the open-loop symmetric flutter boundary. Researchers conducted several of these demonstrations at or below 260 psf and also demonstrated one rolling maneuver at 275 psf, achieving dynamic pressures from 11 percent to 17 percent above the symmetric flutter boundary for all four combinations of control laws.[22]

The numerous successes of the AFW wind tunnel program included validation of the experimental control laws, development of the digital controller, and design and execution of two simulation methods. The control architecture used

---

20. Ibid.

21. Ibid

22. Ibid.

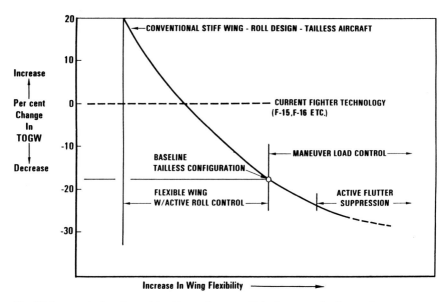

The AFW concept offered a variety of technology payoffs in the areas of roll control, maneuver loads, and flutter suppression. (NASA)

in the 1986 entry was identical to that later used for the full-scale aircraft flight control laws.[23] Additionally, data generated during the 1989 wind tunnel test revealed that RMS control-surface activity predicted by simulation was much higher than those experienced in the wind tunnel. By subsequently making turbulence intensities a function of dynamic pressure, researchers were able to bring simulation-predicted RMS levels into agreement with observed data.[24]

The flight control configuration used on the AFW model served as the basis for further developments. In July 1990, Rockwell engineer Jan Tulinius submitted a patent application for an AFW aircraft control system that featured flexible wings with attached leading- and trailing-edge control surfaces, sensors to measure selected aircraft flight parameters, a system that received and processed pilot command inputs and signals from the sensors, and mechanisms to control the wings in response to processed data. AFW system capabilities included improved aircraft stability and control, optimized cruise and maneuvering performance, as well as augmentation for maneuver load control, gust load alleviation, and flutter suppression. The patent was approved on January 21, 1992.[25]

23. Ibid.

24. Buttrill and Houck, "Hot-Bench Simulation of the Active Flexible Wing Wind-Tunnel Model."

25. Jan Tulinius, "Active Flexible Wing Aircraft Control System," United States Patent 5,082,207, January 21, 1992.

Studies and Proposals

Over the next several years, officials at the Air Force Wright Laboratories (AFWL)—the name was changed in the early 1990s—pursued AFW technology transfer opportunities with several aerospace giants including Rockwell, Boeing, and Lockheed Martin. When researchers from the Air Force and General Dynamics investigated a larger wing design for the F-16 under a program called Agile Falcon, wind tunnel model tests indicated substantial benefits could be derived from including AFW technology.[26] In 1993, Boeing submitted a $12 million proposal to the Advanced Research Projects Agency (ARPA) to design and evaluate AAW technology for use in the proposed High-Speed Civil Transport, a supersonic airliner concept that was ultimately canceled before ever reaching the hardware stage. Boeing had planned to partner with AFWL and NASA Langley, but ARPA declined to fund the company's proposal.[27]

By 1994, several companies were working to develop a new fighter plane under the Joint Advanced Strike Technology (JAST) program. JAST eventually culminated in the Joint Strike Fighter (JSF) competition, a fly-off between two technology demonstrators. The winning competitor received the prime contract to build a replacement for the F-16, which had been in service since the 1970s. Under contract to AFWL in 1994, both Rockwell and Lockheed Martin conducted AFW design methodology studies involving models of JAST-type aircraft. As part of a technology transfer agreement, Rockwell provided Lockheed Martin with an AFW wing for conducting design studies. Lockheed's butterfly-tail concept demonstrated a potential 7-percent reduction in TOGW; Rockwell's tailless concept provided a potential 10-percent reduction. In addition to weight reduction, application of AFW technology also offered improved maneuverability.[28]

Based on the success of the earlier TDT testing, researchers were ready to move forward to the next logical step. According to Ken Griffin, who served as chief of the Structures Division in AFRL's Air Vehicle Directorate, AAW engineers saw significant benefits to be gained from full-scale flight demonstration. "One of

Rockwell's baseline lightweight fighter concept was a tailless airplane with AFW technology for roll control. (NASA)

---

26. Edmund W. Pendleton, Mark Lee, and Lee Wasserman, "Application of Active Flexible Wing Technology to the Agile falcon," *Journal of Aircraft* 29, no. 3 (May–June 1992).

27. Notes on "Active Aeroelastic Wing (AAW) Technology Previous Efforts/Opportunities."

28. Ibid.

the limitations of aeroelastic wind tunnel models comes from the structural scaling required to get the desired flexibility," he noted. "This precludes examining the AAW technology with the wings loaded as in maneuvering flight. We needed to demonstrate it in full scale, full Reynolds Number, with positive-g air loads, actual Mach effects, real flight dynamic pressures, etc. Only with full-scale aircraft flight-testing could we gain all those para-meters in correct scale simultaneously."[29]

Initial proposals defined several requirements for the test bed airplane. It had to have both subsonic and supersonic flight capability. It would need to be equipped with a wing having a minimum of two leading-edge and two trailing-edge control surfaces. The airplane's wing geometry and elastic characteristics had to exhibit trailing-edge roll control reversal. Finally, the airplane had to have provisions for carriage and launch of external stores. The stores carriage provision was eventually deleted, and the capability to fly beyond trailing-edge control reversal was cancelled after early flight tests indicated that this requirement could not be met. To reduce program costs, researchers primarily looked at existing lightweight fighters and research aircraft as test bed candidates.[30]

As researchers moved closer to full-scale flight demonstration, the term Active Flexible Wing was changed to Active Aeroelastic Wing in order to counter the misperception that "flexible" was synonymous with "wimpy" (i.e., lack of structural strength).[31] In one of the earliest informal studies, a Rockwell design study explored the suitability of using one of the company's two X-31 supersonic research aircraft as an AAW technology demonstrator, but this approach was abandoned following the crash of an X-31 at Edwards in January 1995. The airplane was completing its final flight in the joint U.S.-German Enhanced Fighter Maneuverability program, and it would have been available for the AAW project. The second X-31 was already committed to the Navy's VECTOR project.[32]

Subsequently, Rockwell participated in two AAW test bed studies contracted by AFWL in 1995. The objective of the first, led by Lockheed Martin, was to

29. Kenneth Griffin, personal communication to author, November 14, 2012.

30. Robert Clarke, Michael J. Allen, Ryan P. Dibley, Joseph Gera, and John Hodgkinson, "Flight Test of the F/A-18 Active Aeroelastic Wing Airplane," NASA Dryden Flight Research Center, NASA TM-2005-213664 (August 2005).

31. Ed Pendleton, personal communication to author, November 14, 2012.

32. Bob Anderson, Eric Reichenbach, Ron Hess, Ken Griffin, Pete Flick, Dana Purifoy, Denis Bessette, Larry Myers, Dave Voracek, John Baca, Marty Brenner, Bill Lokos, Jim Guffey, Dave Riley, and Ed Pendleton, "Summary of Lessons Learned from the Active Aeroelastic Wing Flight Research Program," draft copy, May 2005.

The X-31 was an early candidate for use in the AAW flight research program, but this plan was abandoned following the loss of the only available airframe. (NASA)

assess potential goals, costs, and benefits of an AAW flight demonstration using a modified F-16. Researchers at NASA Dryden were invited to participate, as well. Dryden acquired an F-16A from NASA Langley, and Lockheed Martin officials wrote a statement of work defining the requirements for converting the airframe into an AAW demonstrator, with an option for additional flight control system (FCS) control modes for follow-on flight research. Plans called for replacing the wing skins with thinner-gauge material for increased flexibility and adding outboard ailerons and independent outboard/inboard leading-edge flaps.[33]

Researchers proposed upgrading the demonstration aircraft to include a Development Block 40 digital flight control computer with a Flight Control Expansion Box to handle additional input/output signals. Improvements to the airplane's operational flight program software would allow the test bed to be flown to desired test conditions using conventional F-16 control laws. The

---

33. Lockheed Martin, "LMTAS Statement of Work for F-16 Active Aeroelastic Wing Flight Demonstration Program," Lockheed Martin Tactical Aircraft Systems, Fort Worth, TX, 1995, provided by Dave Voracek, NASA Dryden Flight Research Center, from personal files.

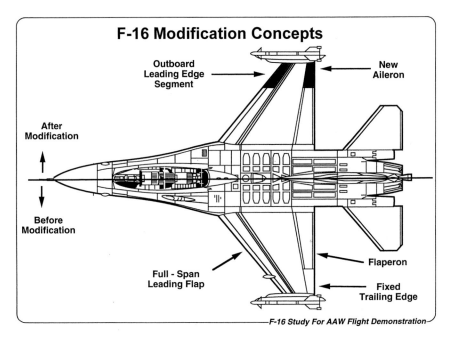

F-16 Modification Concepts

Outboard Leading Edge Segment

New Aileron

After Modification

Before Modification

Full - Span Leading Flap

Flaperon

Fixed Trailing Edge

F-16 Study For AAW Flight Demonstration

Researchers proposed modifying an F-16A for AAW flight research with the addition of outboard control surfaces on the leading and trailing edges of the wing. (NASA)

pilot would then activate the AAW control laws through a panel that allowed manual adjustments to gains.[34]

The team estimated that the project would entail approximately 12 months of detailed design work, 18 months of manufacturing (not including long-lead items), 6 months for ground tests and instrumentation, 12 months of flight-testing, and 6 months for drafting final reports. It was suggested that Lockheed Martin's Tactical Aircraft Systems division in Fort Worth, TX, would assume responsibility for all aircraft modification activities and fabrication of structural components. Rockwell provided consultation on the design concept, aerodynamic modeling, and control law synthesis, and it served as lead for loads model development. NASA Dryden was designated the responsible test organization (RTO) with support from the Air Force Flight Test Center (AFFTC).[35]

The feasibility study showed the viability of improving roll performance by adding outboard leading-edge control surfaces to the F-16 and reducing wing stiffness to improve the airplane's suitability for achieving aileron reversal. The

---

34. Ibid.

35. Ibid.

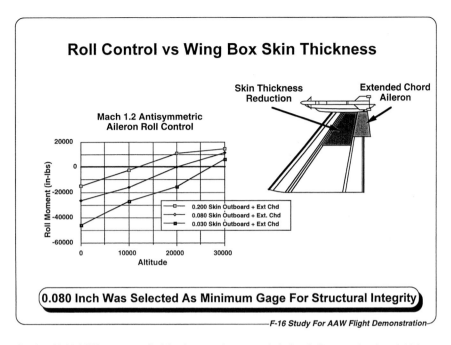

Roll Control vs Wing Box Skin Thickness

Skin Thickness Reduction

Extended Chord Aileron

Mach 1.2 Antisymmetric Aileron Roll Control

Roll Moment (in-lbs)

20000

0

-20000

-40000

-60000

0   10000   20000   30000

Altitude

- 0.200 Skin Outboard + Ext Chd
- 0.080 Skin Outboard + Ext. Chd
- 0.030 Skin Outboard + Ext Chd

0.080 Inch Was Selected As Minimum Gage For Structural Integrity

F-16 Study For AAW Flight Demonstration

Another F-16 AAW concept called for the use of an extended-chord aileron and reduced thickness of the skin panels covering the outer wing box. (NASA)

cost of modifications included the addition of outboard ailerons and outboard leading-edge control surfaces to each wing. Additionally, since the AFFTC operated as an industrial funded organization unless otherwise negotiated, estimates indicated that industrial funding of program activities at the AFFTC would have added substantially to flight-test costs. By the end of the study, Lockheed Martin had offered no proposal in response to the Air Force solicitation for a flight demonstration.[36]

A second Air Force–sponsored joint design study, undertaken in 1995 between Rockwell and McDonnell Douglas, explored the suitability of modifying an F-18 Hornet supersonic aircraft as an AAW technology demonstrator. The preproduction Hornet's aeroelastic characteristics had been identified during testing but had not been considered beneficial at the time. To counteract roll reversal, McDonnell Douglas engineers redesigned the wing structure in a program known as Roll Mod 1. The wings on production model F-18 airframes were torsionally stiffened by replacing multiple upper and lower skin panels

---

36. Anderson et al., "Summary of Lessons Learned from the Active Aeroelastic Wing Flight Research Program."

with fewer and stiffer panels, and by thickening the wing spar. Additionally, the aileron was lengthened and the trailing-edge flap was made to operate as a roll effector. Flight-testing indicated that Roll Mod 1 provided only a moderate improvement in roll performance.[37]

A new set of control laws, known as Roll Mod 2, greatly improved roll power by employing the leading-edge flaps as low-actuation-rate roll effectors during high-speed flight. Some members of the F-18 design team initially rejected this idea because leading-edge control surfaces are considered poor control effectors on stiff or nearly rigid wings. On a relatively flexible wing, use of leading-edge control surfaces at high speeds results in twisting of the entire wing, which produces large roll control forces. It was this characteristic that led researchers to consider the preproduction F-18 wing configuration an ideal tool for demonstrating the AAW concept.[38]

The McDonnell Douglas study considered modifying a NASA F-18 previously used for the High-Alpha Research Vehicle (HARV) program because it was a preproduction prototype with the original wing configuration. As with the F-16 proposal, the Air Force Research Laboratory's Air Vehicles Directorate (formerly AFWAL) would lead the design of the experiment via the aircraft modification effort. NASA Dryden would conduct the flight research program. NASA Langley, AFFTC, and the Naval Weapons Development Center would provide additional support to varying degrees. McDonnell Douglas would modify the aircraft. As subcontractors, Boeing North American (formerly Rockwell) would develop control laws, Moog would develop actuators, and Lockheed Sanders would make changes to the F-18 flight control computer. McDonnell Douglas would develop the flight qualified AFW controller and support Dryden's work with air vehicle systems, simulation, and testing.[39]

The aircraft used for HARV was the sixth preproduction F-18 airframe off the assembly line. It had flexible high-aspect-ratio wings equipped with multiple independent leading- and trailing-edge control surfaces that allowed implementation of AAW control laws without too many structural or control system hardware modifications. The HARV aircraft was also a good candidate for the project because it was already equipped with a research flight control

---

37. Eric Reichenbach, "Explanation of AAW Wing Torsional Stiffness Test Results and Impact on Achieving AAW Flight Research Objectives," November 2001, provided by Dave Voracek, NASA Dryden Flight Research Center, from personal files.

38. Ibid.

39. M.J. McKay, Memo, "Active Flexible Wing Technology Flight Test Demonstration Proposal 94-1028," Rockwell International, North American Aircraft Division, February 25, 1994, provided by Dave Voracek, NASA Dryden Flight Research Center, from personal files.

The F-18 High-Alpha Research Vehicle (HARV) was suggested as a test bed candidate because it was a preproduction airframe with the original wing configuration and was already equipped with a research flight control system. (NASA)

system (RFCS) overlaid with the basic FCS. This allowed for safe testing of new flight research control laws without the need to develop new control laws for takeoff, landing, and basic flight maneuvers. The ability to switch back to the basic FCS from the RFCS provided additional safety. Researchers at Dryden had a great deal of experience with flying the HARV aircraft as well as access to existing facilities for validating control laws and testing the aircraft's systems.[40]

The F-18 AAW feasibility study demonstrated the viability of adding an actuation system to a standard F-18 to independently drive the leading- and trailing-edge control surfaces. Engineers noted that the existing control-surface arrangement met all AAW requirements with relatively minor modifications. Wing structures manufactured for the preproduction F-18 prototypes had

40. S.L. White, "Active Flexible Wing Technology Demonstration: A Proposal in Response to NASA Research Announcement NRA-94-0A-02—Advanced Concepts for Aeronautics," Rockwell International, North American Aircraft Division, February 25, 1994, provided by Dave Voracek, NASA Dryden Flight Research Center, from personal files.

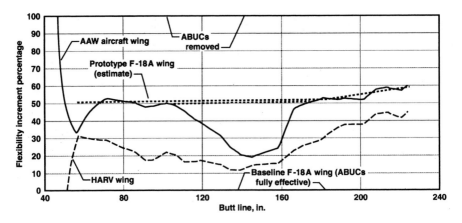

This graph compares the flexibility of the HARV wing to that of the planned AAW wing configuration, including the effect of removing the aft box upper cover (ABUC) panel. (NASA)

stiffness levels exceptionally suitable for the AAW demonstration. In addition, the F-18 flight control computer (FCC) was ideally suited to AAW flight-control law implementation and development. Cost of all modifications was initially estimated at approximately $8 million, which was significantly less expensive than the F-16 option.[41]

Early studies yielded only very rough estimates, and numerous factors influenced final program costs. Boeing acquired McDonnell Douglas through a 1997 merger prior to the full-scale AAW flight demonstration program. Overall F-18 AAW modification costs on an Air Force contract eventually rose to $9.282 million for work performed by Boeing but not including the cost of ground- or flight-testing. Completion of wing hydraulic plumbing and instrumentation resulted in additional NASA costs.[42]

In the long run, researchers and program advocates considered the expense a relative bargain. In a memo to AFWL program manager Ed Pendleton, Dryden's AAW flight project manager Denis E. Bessette wrote, "We think this program will provide flight research that can lead to significant improvements in performance and economy of future aircraft, both military and civilian."[43]

---

41. Anderson et al., "Summary of Lessons Learned from the Active Aeroelastic Wing Flight Research Program."

42. Ibid.

43. Denis E. Bessette, Memo re: "Assignment of Dryden Aircraft to the Active Aeroelastic Wing (AAW) Program," n.d., circa 1995, provided by Dave Voracek, NASA Dryden Flight Research Center, from personal files.

Aircraft Modifications

The joint flight research effort among Air Force, NASA, Navy, and industry participants to demonstrate key characteristics of AAW technology was
officially initiated in January 1996. As had been proposed, NASA Dryden
hosted the flight-test program and also provided the test bed, NASA 840, the
preproduction F-18 (Navy Bu. No. 160780) that had previously been used
for the HARV project. The aircraft first had to be demodified from the HARV
configuration. This meant removal of thrust-vectoring vanes from the engine
exhaust, ballast weights, and a spin chute fixture that had been used during
high-angle-of-attack research flights. The original engine exhaust nozzles would
need to be reinstalled, along with a hardware box to allow the RFCS to operate
without the thrust-vectoring vanes. Technicians at Dryden planned to install
strain gauges for bending and torsion moments. These would be calibrated by
loading the wings to simulate specific flight loads for various flight conditions.[44]

In August 1996, following a competitive award process, the Air Vehicles
Directorate and NASA Dryden awarded a contract to McDonnell Douglas for
modification of the F-18 aircraft to make it suitable as an AAW demonstrator.
NASA maintained an existing F-18 support contract with McDonnell Douglas
to support changes needed to support flight-test operations at Dryden. The
$15 million Air Force contract included modifying the wing to preproduction
stiffness levels, adding trailing-edge outboard control-surface actuation, developing AAW control laws at Boeing North American, autocoding of control
laws, and making changes to the flight control computer. The original F-18
wing structure included three skin panels on both the upper and lower surfaces
inboard of the wing fold.[45] The outboard portion of the wing had one upper
surface panel and two lower surface panels. The skin panels were constructed of
aluminum, titanium, and carbon fiber composite materials. On the modified
wing, the three upper surface panels on the inboard section were replaced with
five panels made of aluminum and thinner composite skins with honeycomb
substructure. On the outboard portion of the wing, the single composite upper
surface panel was replaced with two thinner aluminum panels and one thinner
composite skin panel. The NASA support contract provided money maintaining F-18 airworthiness, developing software for verification and validation of

---

44. S.L. White, "Active Flexible Wing Technology Demonstration: A Proposal in Response to NASA
    Research Announcement NRA-94-0A-02 – Advanced concepts for Aeronautics."

45. As on many Navy airplanes, the wings of the F-18 were equipped with a hinge that allowed them
    to be folded when the aircraft was parked so that the aircraft took up less space on the deck or
    hangar areas of an aircraft carrier.

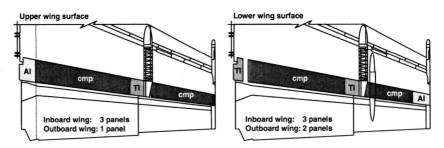

Original aircraft wing panel configuration.

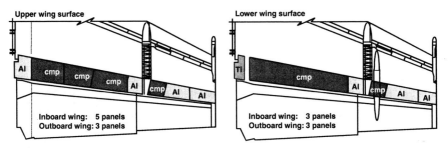

Modified AAW aircraft wing panel configuration.

In order to increase the flexibility of the AAW wings, large skin panels from the original configuration were replaced with several smaller panels. (NASA)

control laws, and conducting flight operations. Boeing acquired McDonnell Douglas, including its Phantom Works organization, through a 1997 merger, but this had no effect on the AAW program.[46]

As Phantom Works technicians began inspecting NASA 840, they discovered cracks on the airframe near where the twin vertical tails joined the aft fuselage. Boeing inspectors recommended not flying the airplane for AAW testing until the cracked components and any associated damage were repaired. Original preproduction hardware was no longer available, and the current production equivalent was significantly different in terms of configuration and materials. The differences would have affected interchangeability and structural loading and would have necessitated replacement of other adjacent assemblies. Before any of this occurred, significant teardown and inspection, followed by

---

46. Ed Pendleton, Dave Voracek, Eric Reichenbach, and Kenneth Griffin, "The X-53: A Summary of the Active Aeroelastic Wing Flight Research Program," AIAA-2007-1855, 48th AIAA/ASME/ASCE/AHS/ASC Structures, Structural Dynamics, and Materials Conference, Honolulu, Hawaii, April 2007.

Researchers ultimately selected a production F-18 for modification as the AAW flight research test bed. (NASA)

extensive engineering analysis, was necessary to quantify the impact of these changes.[47]

Denis Bessette judged that the proposed repair costs and schedule delays were prohibitive. He recommended using a different F-18 and simply exchanging its production-type wings for those of NASA 840.[48] The replacement test bed airframe was a production model F-18 (Navy Bu. No. 161744) that had resided at Dryden since March 1999 as NASA 853. Technicians exchanged the wings of NASA 853 with those of NASA 840 in order to obtain the required level of torsional stiffness, but optimal demonstration of AAW technology required additional modifications. These included replacement of the wing skin with thinner panels designed to increase flexibility and installation of a system that drove the outboard and inboard leading-edge

---

47. Peter B. Field, Eric Y. Reichenbach, Robert C. Anderson, Oliver K. Hall, Ronald K. Hess, Steven H. Goldthorpe, Nicholas J. Lapointe, and Thomas C. Nurczyk, "The Active Aeroelastic Wing (AAW) Flight Research Program, the X-53—Final Report," Air Force Research Laboratory, Air Vehicles Directorate, AFRL-VA-WP-TR-2005-3082 (August 2005).

48. Ed Pendleton, personal communication to author, July 9, 2012.

flaps independently. The test bed was also equipped with new flight control computer hardware and software and a research instrumentation system to monitor aircraft dynamics and loads.[49]

Special instrumentation was required for gathering data on aeroelastic effects. Lead avionics technician Jim Mills, along with Dallas Quantz, Mark Nicholson, and several Air Force technicians, pulled all the panels off the aircraft and installed approximately 400 sensors, producing a wire bundle 3 inches thick. They also sought assistance from the aerodynamicists in determining weight and size restrictions and placement of sensors and wires. Lead AAW instrumentation engineer Joe Hernandez and his group reviewed requests from various project teams before deciding where to place the numerous sensors and miles of wire. Not every request could be accommodated.[50]

"You can have requests for 20,000 parameters, but there's not enough real estate on the aircraft," Hernandez said in a 2003 interview. "We let them know what they can have and what they can't."[51]

The final instrumentation package measured more than 1,600 independent parameters during ground and flight tests. Technicians installed 200 strain gages to monitor control-surface hinge moments and wing root/fold loads. Wing displacement and twist were measured with 16 deflection sensors, and there were 50 dynamic accelerometers that enabled flutter testing and structural dynamics research. Each control surface was equipped with two position sensors in addition to those normally included on the aircraft. This allowed engineers to track spanwise elastic warping of the control surfaces. The instrumentation package also included sensors to monitor temperatures and FCC commands, as well as accelerometers to measure roll, pitch, and yaw. Aircraft health-monitoring functions were executed by the mission computer, and a set of pressure taps behind the outboard leading-edge flap collected unsteady pressure measurements.[52]

Use of the leading-edge flaps as maneuvering control surfaces necessitated development of improved control actuators. The leading-edge flap drive system (LEFDS) on the production F-18 aircraft controls both the inboard

---

49. Pendleton, Voracek, Reichenbach, and Griffin, "The X-53: A Summary of the Active Aeroelastic Wing Flight Research Program."

50. Jay Levine, "Key Roles: AAW taps into Dryden's knowledge, experience and flight research savvy," *X-Press*, Special Active Aeroelastic Wing Edition, NASA Dryden Flight Research Center (December 17, 2003): p. 2.

51. Ibid., p. 2.

52. Pendleton, Voracek, Reichenbach, and Griffin, "The X-53: A Summary of the Active Aeroelastic Wing Flight Research Program."

From left to right, technicians Bob Fleckenstein, Andre Sentif, and Mark Nicholson work with crew chief Daryl Townsend (lower right) to install instrumentation on AAW wing. (Jim Mills)

and outboard leading-edge flaps as a single unit. AAW project engineers at the Phantom Works and technicians at Moog Aircraft Group in Torrance, CA, modified the LEFDS to enable the inboard and outboard leading-edge control surfaces to deflect independently of one another and modified the control-surface travel limits.[53]

Technicians at Dryden removed the wings from NASA 840 and shipped them to the Boeing Phantom Works in February 1999. There, the wing skins were replaced with more flexible panels, and documented and undocumented damage, such as composite delamination, wire chafing, elongated fastener holes, and valve leakage, was repaired. Boeing technicians completed structural, hydraulic, and electrical modifications, but they were unable to install the LEFDS because a complete system was not yet available. The remaining work was subsequently finished at Dryden after the wings were returned to NASA in March 2000.[54]

---

53. Ibid.

54. Field et al., "The Active Aeroelastic Wing (AAW) Flight Research Program, the X-53—Final Report."

AAW INSTRUMENTATION - SENSORS

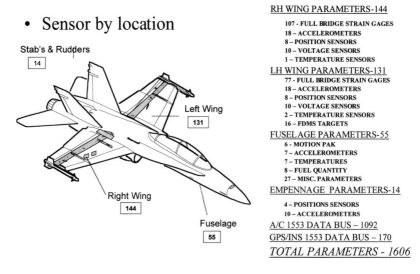

- ## Sensor by location

Stab's & Rudders
14

Left Wing
131

Right Wing
144

Fuselage
55

RH WING PARAMETERS-144
- 107 - FULL BRIDGE STRAIN GAGES
- 18 – ACCELEROMETERS
- 8 – POSITION SENSORS
- 10 – VOLTAGE SENSORS
- 1 – TEMPERATURE SENSORS

LH WING PARAMETERS-131
- 77 - FULL BRIDGE STRAIN GAGES
- 18 – ACCELEROMETERS
- 8 – POSITION SENSORS
- 10 – VOLTAGE SENSORS
- 2 – TEMPERATURE SENSORS
- 16 – FDMS TARGETS

FUSELAGE PARAMETERS-55
- 6 - MOTION PAK
- 7 – ACCELEROMETERS
- 7 – TEMPERATURES
- 8 – FUEL QUANTITY
- 27 – MISC. PARAMETERS

EMPENNAGE PARAMETERS-14
- 4 – POSITIONS SENSORS
- 10 – ACCELEROMETERS

A/C 1553 DATA BUS – 1092
GPS/INS 1553 DATA BUS – 170

TOTAL PARAMETERS - 1606

Sensors installed in the airplane's wings, fuselage, and tail surfaces recorded more than 1,600 parameters. (NASA)

LE Flap Drive System (LEFDS) Mods

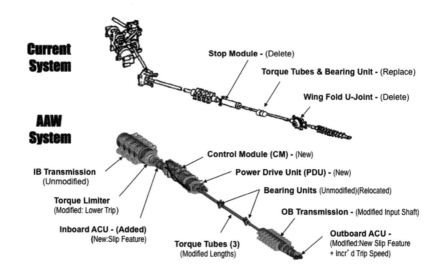

Current System

Stop Module - (Delete)

Torque Tubes & Bearing Unit - (Replace)

Wing Fold U-Joint - (Delete)

AAW System

Control Module (CM) - (New)

Power Drive Unit (PDU) - (New)

Bearing Units (Unmodified)(Relocated)

OB Transmission - (Modified Input Shaft)

IB Transmission (Unmodified)

Torque Limiter (Modified: Lower Trip)

Inboard ACU - (Added) (New:Slip Feature)

Torque Tubes (3) (Modified Lengths)

Outboard ACU - (Modified:New Slip Feature + Incr' d Trip Speed)

This diagram compares the standard F-18 leading-edge flap drive system with the LEFDS used for the X-53, indicating the necessary modifications. (Boeing)

In November 1997, Boeing and NASA contracted Lockheed Martin Control Systems (subsequently acquired by BAE Systems in April 2000) in Binghamton, NY, to design, develop, build, test, and deliver the test bed's FCC system. The basic FCC on an F-18 consists of a quadruplex redundant system that maintains control of the aircraft, manages actuator signal input and output, communicates with the aircraft's mission computer, and displays information through a Military Standard 1553 Data Bus with four Analog 6 cards. The contract initially called for delivery of one ship set of AAW FCCs, and NASA supplied two FCCs (previously modified for the HARV program) as Government-furnished equipment. Software design requirements for the AAW tests resulted in modifications that provided an additional analog interface to drive the outboard leading-edge flaps and a faster processor to accommodate AAW software for the RFCS.[55]

In June 1998, after NASA officials realized how difficult it would be to maintain the planned testing schedule with only one ship set of computers, Lockheed Martin was authorized to build a second one. The HARV FCC had been modified to include a pilot-selectable research control law processor, and it spawned development of a production support flight control computer (PSFCC) for use in later model F-18 aircraft. The PSFCC featured a research flight control processor that was piggybacked onto the baseline FCC to allow the use of conventional control laws for all phases of flight, as well as research control laws for specified areas of the flight envelope.[56]

For the AAW FCC, Lockheed Martin technicians built upon the previous HARV and PSFCC efforts. Under NASA contract, the company designed and built both ship sets, each with four 68040 processor cards similar to those used on the F-15 Advanced Control Technology for Integrated Vehicles (ACTIVE) test bed. The ACTIVE processor board's bus structure was incompatible with that of the AAW FCC and required redesign. Lockheed Martin technicians used this opportunity to make a number of enhancements including increased RAM and flash memory, increased ability to handle multiple interrupts, the addition of seven software programmable timers, and the addition of a MIL-STD-1553 protocol chip.[57]

The standard FCC processor ran baseline F-18 flight control laws and computed commands for all control surfaces including the new outboard

---

55. Ibid.

56. John Carter and Mark Stephenson, "Initial Flight Test of the Production Support Flight Control Computers at NASA Dryden Flight Research Center," NASA TM-1999-206581 (August 1999).

57. Field et al., "The Active Aeroelastic Wing (AAW) Flight Research Program, the X-53—Final Report."

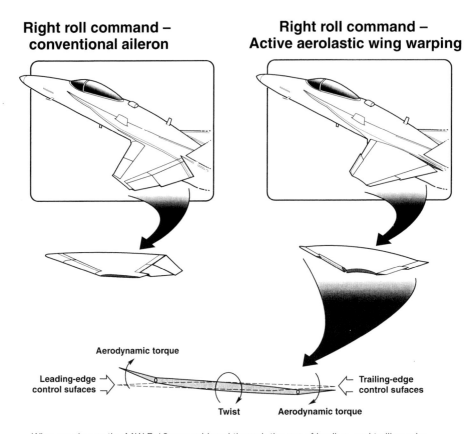

Right roll command – conventional aileron

Right roll command – Active aerolastic wing warping

Aerodynamic torque

Leading-edge control sufaces

Trailing-edge control sufaces

Twist   Aerodynamic torque

Wing warping on the AAW F-18 was achieved through the use of leading- and trailing-edge control surfaces to generate aerodynamic torque. (NASA)

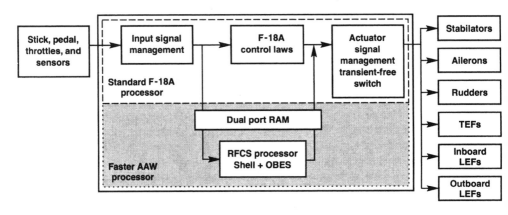

This schematic illustrates the system architecture of the F-18 flight control computer. (NASA)

leading-edge flap. The RFCS communicated with the FCC through a dual-port random access memory, and it had no direct control of the aircraft. Used only during research portions of AAW flights, it provided a flexible system for control law research. During test flights, the pilot selected a preprogrammed maneuver from the cockpit display and then engaged the RFCS by pushing a button on the control stick. When this system was engaged, actuator commands computed by the RFCS replaced commands from the baseline FCC. When the RFCS disengaged, intentionally or through malfunction, transition logic reverted flight control back to the baseline FCC.[58]

Several significant difficulties were encountered during FCC modification. First, Lockheed Martin's original proposal called for adding between 50 and 60 jumper wires to the Analog 6 card in each channel of the FCC, but the original HARV cards already had 50 such wires. As a result, the cost estimate for modifying the cards increased. Although new Analog 6 cards would have cost slightly more than modified cards, AAW program managers decided it would be better to procure new ones rather than modify the HARV cards. Interface wiring for the new outboard leading-edge-flap actuators was installed on boards previously used for the HARV thrust-vectoring vane actuators. Since the vanes had not been flight critical, they were not subject to built-in test (BIT). But because the AAW leading-edge flaps were flight critical and required continuous power-up BIT (PBIT), the FCC required additional wiring changes to provide that capability. There were also concerns that the 68040 chip would draw so much electric current that the FCC power supply would not operate over the full range of input voltage. During discussions in the summer of 1998, program managers determined that, short of a dual generator failure, there was very little risk that input voltage would drop below operational levels.[59]

BAE Systems performed acceptance testing on the FCCs prior to delivery of the ship sets. Beyond the standard F-18 FCC Acceptance Test Procedures, this included vibration testing, environmental stress screening, and a manual engineering test procedure to verify AAW-unique changes to the FCC. Testing the parameter identification (PID) software with Ship Set No. 1 revealed a memory problem that required returning the 68040 chip to BAE for reprogramming. Since it was considered a hardware failure, BAE sent the chip back to the manufacturer for replacement of the failed unit. When BAE was ready

---

58. Pendleton, Voracek, Reichenbach, and Griffin, "The X-53: A Summary of the Active Aeroelastic Wing Flight Research Program."

59. Field et al., "The Active Aeroelastic Wing (AAW) Flight Research Program, the X-53—Final Report."

to reprogram the chip, the company's equipment was not available, so the chip was sent to an outside vendor. Programming errors resulted in more apparent failures, but the actual cause was not discovered until after the three original 68040 cards had been programmed with two minor errors that required patching. BAE provided the patch software, and Boeing installed it. The chips were successfully debugged, but the entire process cost the program a month of extra work. Further delays resulted from Navy requirements for qualification testing of the 68040 chip that were more stringent than those used by NASA during the F-15 ACTIVE program. This meant another 4-week delay in shipping the FCCs to Boeing.[60]

Another problem cropped up when the Dryden team discovered that Ship Set No. 2 would operate only when the ground service equipment (GSE) power generator was turned on. After Boeing returned Ship Set No. 1 from St. Louis, NASA verified that it worked properly and sent the other FCC back to BAE for troubleshooting. BAE technicians were unable to determine the nature of the problem until they examined both FCCs and found a disparity in the dual-port RAM processor registers. Minor frame overruns in the 68040 processors caused Ship Set No. 2 to enter Fault Shutdown mode. Oddly, although Ship Set No. 2 had the proper component, turning the GSE on disabled the cache memory. Ship Set No. 1 had been equipped with the wrong part, but the dual-port RAM timing was not an issue, and the FCC worked. The two components were physically identical but had slightly different part numbers, a subtle difference that had been missed during quality assurance checks. In order to avoid further delays in the flight-testing schedule, and since the PID software did not require cache memory, the cache memory was disabled as a temporary solution. BAE waited until the end of Phase 1 testing to implement a final solution that required a variety of hardware and software changes.[61]

Several additional modifications were required in order to finish work on the AAW test bed. First, it was equipped with an aluminum nose cone that had been previously flown on the HARV aircraft because it was modified to support a flight-test nose boom that provided more precise air data. Cockpit modifications included the addition of RFCS controls and an Air Force–type oxygen system interface to make the airplane compatible with the rest of Dryden's F-18 fleet. The electronics bay (E-Bay), just aft of the cockpit, was modified to hold research instrumentation. Finally, a special fairing, designed by Tony

---

60. Ibid.
61. Ibid.

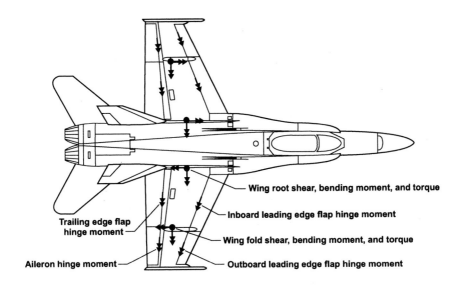

Wing root shear, bending moment, and torque

Inboard leading edge flap hinge moment

Trailing edge flap
hinge moment

Wing fold shear, bending moment, and torque

Aileron hinge moment

Outboard leading edge flap hinge moment

Strain gauges and other instrumentation measured component loads on the airplane's wings and control surfaces. (NASA)

Chen and built at Dryden, was mounted on top of the upper fuselage spine to house a flight-deflection measurement system (FDMS).[62]

Traditionally, flight-load measurement on aircraft structures has been done using metallic-resistance strain gauges that are physically bonded along key elements of the structural load paths. Applied loads cause structural members to deform (strain), producing an electrical resistance charge in the gauge that is proportional to the load. As an alternative to mechanical strain gauges, researchers at NASA Langley investigated an optical technique for remotely measuring the relationship between macroscopic deflection of the aircraft structure and the corresponding flight loads. The AAW flight-test program provided a unique opportunity to demonstrate deflection-based load estimation using data from the FDMS. Technicians installed 16 infrared light-emitting diodes on the upper surface of the airplane's left wing to serve as targets for two receivers inside the FDMS fairing. During Phase 1 flight testing, researchers compared estimated loads based on deflection to measured loads based on strain. They found a strong correlation in regard to bending moment, and a slightly weaker torque correlation, because high toque loads are not always

---

62. Mauricio Rivas, "Active Aeroelastic Wing Project Dryden Independent Review, Flight Operations Engineering," briefing to AAW Flight Readiness Review Board, March 2002, provided by Dave Voracek, NASA Dryden Flight Research Center, from personal files.

associated with large structural deflections. Additionally, they suggested that although strain gauges are a highly reliable load measurement device, use of deflection-based measurement systems would reduce aircraft weight and test preparation time and be easier to install, improving aircraft performance and lowering operational costs.[63]

Structural Analysis and Ground Testing

Prior to flight testing, researchers at Dryden conducted extensive aircraft structural analysis and ground testing to mitigate risks and prepare the airplane for flight. These preparations included wing torsional stiffness measurements, loads calibration, ground vibration tests, and structural mode interaction studies. A preliminary torsional stiffness test performed on the left wing in November 1996 established baseline data on production F-18 wing flexibility with all skin panels in place, as well as with the aft wing box covers removed. A second test series was conducted on the same wing in April 2001 to establish the torsional stiffness characteristics of the modified AAW wing and to provide data for analytical model validation.[64]

The objectives of the second series of wing torsional stiffness tests included establishing the maximum possible torsional flexibility increment that theoretically could be produced as a result of modifying the aft wing box skin panels. Researchers also needed to characterize the modified wing's torsional stiffness and compare it with the baseline data to assess the effectiveness of the modifications. Finally, they needed to validate the repeatability of the testing method and make comparisons with finite element model (FEM) predictions. All testing took place in the Dryden Flight Loads Laboratory (FLL).[65]

The defueled airplane was towed into the FLL on April 2, jacked, and leveled. For the 1996 test, the main landing gear was depressurized, supported with short jacks, and secured to the floor. This time, technicians removed the main landing gear entirely and installed substitute trunnions and side braces

---

63. Andrew M. Lizotte and William A. Lokos, "Deflection-Based Aircraft Structural Loads Estimation with Comparison to Flight," AIAA-2005-2016, presented at the AIAA/ASME/ASCE/AHS/ASC Structures, Structural Dynamics & Materials Conference, Austin, TX, April 18–21, 2005.

64. Pendleton, Voracek, Reichenbach, and Griffin, "The X-53: A Summary of the Active Aeroelastic Wing Flight Research Program."

65. William A. Lokos, Candida D. Olney, Natalie D. Crawford, Rick Stauf, and Erich Y. Reichenbach, "Wing Torsional Stiffness Tests of the Active Aeroelastic Wing F/A-18 Airplane," NASA Dryden Flight Research Center, NASA TM-2002-210723 (May 2002).

The extensively instrumented F-18 airframe was subjected to torsional stiffness and vibration testing in the Dryden Flight Loads Laboratory. The results were critical to the success of the AAW flight research program. (NASA)

as part of the setup for a subsequent loads calibration test.[66] The trunnions were attached to steel H-beam assemblies and bolted to the floor. The nose gear remained in place, attached to the floor with loose safety chains, and the tailhook was replaced with a support fixture and secured to the floor with guy cables. Loading fixtures were installed on the left wing and connected to four loading columns. Data recording instrumentation included string potentiometers installed on the fuselage centerline between the engines, as well as on both horizontal stabilizers and on both main landing gear trunnions for observation of rigid-body movement. The FDMS provided sensor measurements of the left wing upper surface.[67]

---

66. Ibid.

67. Natalie Crawford, "AAW Wing Torsional Stiffness Test Report with Preliminary Findings," NASA AAW-2001-010 (April 2001), provided by Dave Voracek, NASA Dryden Flight Research Center, from personal files.

This multiple exposure emphasizes the wing deflections produced by test fixtures in the FLL. (NASA)

Dave Neufeld (front left), Steve Thomas, and Mark Nunnelee (standing) control and monitor loads testing of the AAW airplane. (NASA)

During torsional stiffness tests, two actuators applied loads in one direction while the other two applied loads in an equal, but opposite, direction. FLL technicians increased loading in steps of 20 percent of the test limit load, allowing ample time between steps for observation and data collection. The first load measurements, made on April 10, 2001, were used for verification of data displays and to check structural and dump responses using 20 percent as the maximum load. Comparison of deflection data with baseline data from the 1996 wing stiffness test showed that AAW wing deflections were considerably lower than expected. After engineers studied differences between the two test configurations that might account for this, they decided to repeat the torsional test with the leading-edge flaps unlocked and the dummy actuators disconnected. When testing resumed the following day, the change had a significant effect, but one still less than expected. Technicians then removed the aft wing box upper skin panel fasteners and performed another load cycle. The subsequent deflection data were very similar to the results of panels-off tests performed in 1996.[68]

Overall, these tests successfully quantified the AAW wing's torsional stiffness for the flight configuration and provided good comparative data between the original production wing and the lighter, more flexible AAW wing. The FDMS provided excellent data for correlating wing deflection and loads. Outstanding teamwork among the aircraft crew, mechanics, and FLL technicians allowed for rapid test setup and execution, saving 1 week of project schedule time.[69] The modified wing was found to be approximately 5 percent more flexible than the baseline F-18 wing and had more torsional stiffness than was predicted using the FEM. Engineers found that the analytical model overpredicted wingtip flexibility by 42 percent and required adjustment using the new data. Once adjusted, the FEM could be used for aeroelasticity predictions and control law development.[70]

The next phase of testing (wing-load calibration) was designed to ensure the development of accurate strain gauge–based load equations and address applied-load design anomalies. There were four objectives. The primary objective was to obtain calibration data from strain gauge instrumentation during the application of single-point and distributed loads. The resulting data served as the basis for loads equations and as a research database for analytical strain gauge calibration work. Second, researchers wished to simultaneously collect measurements from the electro-optical FDMS and ground-test deflection

---

68. Ibid.

69. Ibid.

70. Lokos et al., "Wing Torsional Stiffness Tests of the Active Aeroelastic Wing F/A-18 Airplane."

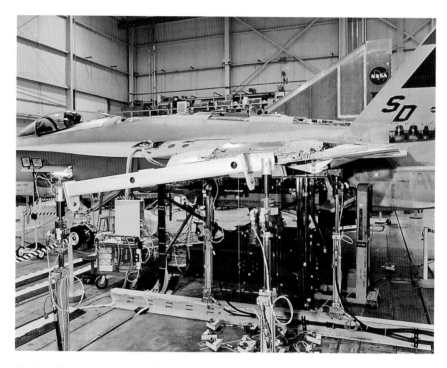

A series of tests in the FLL quantified the AAW wing's torsional stiffness and provided comparative data between the original production wing and the lighter, more flexible research wing. (NASA)

potentiometers for comparison of the two measurement systems. A third objective involved the collection of strain gauge data through both the airplane's pulse code modulation (PCM) data system and the DACS3 data system used in the FLL for signal-to-noise ratio and error analysis. Last, but not least, the team collected overall aircraft wing stiffness data. The complete process was scheduled to take 83 days.[71]

Wing-load calibration tests were made using a test fixture equipped with 32 hydraulic jacks that applied loads through 104 tension and compression pads bonded to the wing surface. Dryden engineers developed load equations for wing root and fold shear, bending moment, torque, and leading-/trailing-edge control-surface hinge moments. They performed 72 load cases (single-point, double-point, and distributed) and compared loads calculated from strain gauge outputs with aggregate applied loads. Load equations based

71. William A. Lokos, "Test Plan for the F-18 AAW (TN853) Wing Strain Gage Loads Calibration Test," NASA Dryden Flight Research Center, March 2001.

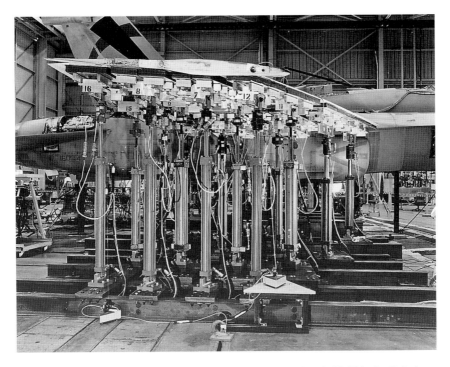

FLL technicians conducted load calibration tests using a fixture equipped with 32 hydraulic jacks that applied loads through 104 tension and compression pads bonded to the wing surface. (NASA)

on the results were later implemented in the control room and monitored in real time during flight tests.[72]

Engineers had calculated the baseline stiffness using assumed values based on a new wing with minimum wear-induced hysteresis. Because the wings from the NASA 840 had experienced significant flight wear that resulted in slippage between panels, fasteners, and substructure, the wing stiffness was not reduced as much as expected. The overall measured stiffness of the AAW wing was calculated to be approximately 5 percent less than that of the baseline F-18 wing with wear and approximately 17 percent less than that of the baseline wing with no wear. The AAW team successfully achieved the goal of returning the production airplane's wing to a stiffness level approaching that of the preproduction model and giving it sufficient flexibility to demonstrate AAW technology.[73]

---

72. Pendleton, Voracek, Reichenbach, and Griffin, "The X-53: A Summary of the Active Aeroelastic Wing Flight Research Program."

73. Ibid.

As part of the structural analysis, aerodynamicists at Boeing and NASA adjusted baseline F-18 data to account for the increase in wing flexibility. Boeing, under AFRL contract, created a finite element model of the F-18 AAW to assess the effects of the wing stiffness tests and then updated it in accordance with test results. Researchers used the FEM to analyze the airplane's aerodynamic characteristics, aeroelastic control power, vibration qualities, structural integrity, design loads, stress, and preliminary flutter analysis.[74]

Because the FEM was used for both static and dynamic aeroelastic analyses, it had to accurately represent the mass and stiffness properties imparted to the wing as a result of structural modifications. Researchers rendered a new model using NASA's Structural Analysis (NASTRAN) finite element analysis program and downsized it using a property averaging process that preserved the substructure layout, aligned elements according to property variations, and retained structure required for attaching the control surfaces. Wing sectional mass data taken from a flight-validated F-18 beam model used for flutter analysis were then distributed to the nodes of the downsized model. Structural and nonstructural mass was distributed to match the sectional mass, center of gravity, and pitch inertia of the AAW wing. Finally, beam models of the leading- and trailing-edge control surfaces and wingtip missile rail were attached to the wing box structural model. A ground vibration test provided values for wing fold and control-surface hinge stiffness.[75]

Two structural configurations were used for testing the wing stiffness model. The baseline test simulated the wing FEM with all structural components installed. For the second test, known as the simulated AAW configuration, the aft wing box upper skins were removed to allow study of the incremental effect of these covers since they would ultimately be replaced with more flexible panels representing the structural modifications. The wing FEM was subsequently adjusted and correlated with the stiffness test data. The correlated wing model was then applied to beam models of the F-18 fuselage and empennage to facilitate collection of flutter data for correlation with ground vibration test results. Researchers developed a final F-18 AAW FEM using the correlated results of stiffness and modal tests and with the addition of the planned aircraft modifications. These included the more flexible skin panels, as well as additional concentrated mass representing the new outboard LEFDS. The model was configured with landing gear retracted, a full fuel load, and elements representing nose boom and wingtip missile rails. Concentrated stiffness elements

---

74. Ibid.

75. Field et al., "The Active Aeroelastic Wing (AAW) Flight Research Program, the X-53—Final Report."

Researchers monitor aeroservoelastic data in Dryden's Structural Analysis Facility. From left (seated): University of California San Diego graduate student Marianne Crowder, Roger Truax, Natalie Crawford, and National Research Council postdoctoral student Chad Prazenica; standing: lead structural engineer Marty Brenner and Structural Dynamics Group leader Chan-Gi Pak. (NASA)

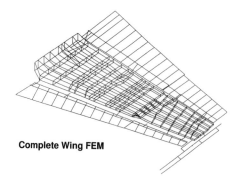

Complete Wing FEM

Researchers developed a finite element model to represent mass and stiffness properties of the F-18 wing. (NASA)

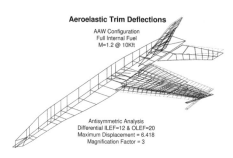

Aeroelastic Trim Deflections

AAW Configuration
Full Internal Fuel
M=1.2 @ 10Kft

Antisymmetric Analysis
Differential ILEF=12 & OLEF=20
Maximum Displacement = 6.418
Magnification Factor = 3

This full airframe structural dynamic model incorporating AAW wing FEM was used to predict aeroelastic trim deflections. (NASA)

represented soft jacks simulating those to be used in vibration tests. Researchers used the results of this aeroelastic modeling and analysis to predict the effects of structural flexibility on the AAW F-18's aerodynamics and structural loads.[76]

In order to validate the analytical model, the test bed airframe was subjected to ground vibration testing (GVT) in the Flight Loads Laboratory at Dryden. Researchers performed the GVT to assess the airplane's dynamic structural characteristics and verify that the structural modifications had been correctly modeled. The results were used to update the computer model for subsequent flutter analysis. The GVT was accomplished by mounting the airplane on a soft jack support system that approximately simulated free flight conditions while isolating the F-18's rigid-body modes from its elastic-structural modes. The airplane was mounted in gear-up flight configuration with the control surfaces in a nulled position. Tests with full and empty fuel tanks were required for validation of the analytical model. Two 150-pound shakers were positioned on the outer torque boxes at the intersection of the spar and rib, along the leading edge of the right wing and the trailing edge of the left wing. A third shaker was attached to the left horizontal stabilator. Random excitation from all three produced a broadband response from the airplane as researchers applied increased force levels to check for nonlinearity. In nearly a dozen cases, GVT mode shapes matched the analytical model's modal frequencies to within 10 percent.[77]

The soft jack support system was also used for structural mode interaction (SMI) tests to verify that vibrations resulting from the structural modifications

---

76. Ibid.

77. Pendleton, Voracek, Reichenbach, and Griffin, "The X-53: A Summary of the Active Aeroelastic Wing Flight Research Program."

Loads Lab technicians including, from left, Dave Dennis, Freddy Graham, and Jeff Doughty position a support cylinder under the right wing of the AAW test aircraft prior to ground vibration testing. (NASA)

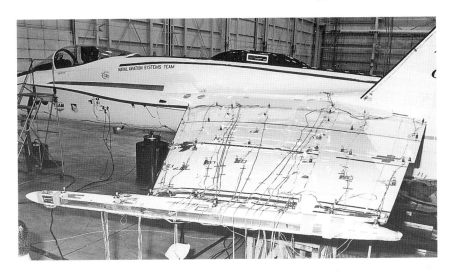

During ground vibration tests, the upper wing surfaces were covered with accelerometers and other sensors. The FDMS pod is visible atop the spine of the airplane above the wing. (NASA)

would not adversely affect the FCS. The results had several applications. First, researchers used SMI data to calculate responses and transfer functions (a mathematical representation of the relation between the input and output of a linear time-invariant system) that defined the dynamic relationship of the airframe and control-surface actuators. Second, they determined whether dynamic coupling occurred between the airframe and the FCS sensors and actuators. The final, and most important, objective was to ensure that all servoelastic gains met safety requirements. The SMI tests consisted of activating the FCS and performing a series of six onboard excitation system (OBES) maneuvers including a symmetric sweep of the ailerons, outboard leading-edge flaps, stabilators, and rudders. Additionally, the ailerons and outboard leading-edge flaps were swept antisymmetrically. During these maneuvers, the airframe was subjected to a combination of numerous sine wave signals of varying frequency (known as Schroeder inputs) for 35 seconds. No adverse interaction between the control system and aircraft structure was found, and the SMI test successfully demonstrated that the AAW test bed had sufficient gain margins for safe operation.[78]

F-18 AAW Wind Tunnel Model

While the F-18 underwent ground testing at Dryden, researchers at Langley were developing methods to validate predictive models and identify critical parameters using an approximately quarter-scale, half-span wind tunnel model. This investigation, culminating in July and August 2004 with testing in Langley's TDT, served AAW program goals in several ways. Data collected in the TDT served as a benchmark for comparison with flight data and other theoretical analyses. It also provided researchers with insight into the effects of various parameters on the vehicle's aeroelastic response. Finally, it provided data to validate scaling laws and their applicability for use with future statically scaled aeroelastic models.[79]

The model, designed and built at Langley, was a 26-percent geometrically scaled, half-span representation of the F-18 right-hand fuselage, wing, and

---

78. Ibid.

79. Jennifer Heeg, Charles V. Spain, James R. Florance, Carol D. Wiesemen, Thomas G. Ivanco, Joshua A. DeMoss, Walter A. Silva, Andrew Panetta, Peter Lively, and Vic Tumwa, "Experimental Results from the Active Aeroelastic Wing Wind Tunnel Test Program," AIAA 2005-2234, presented at the 46th AIAA/ASME/ASCE/AHS/ASC Structures, Structural Dynamics & Materials Conference, Austin, TX, April 18–21, 2005.

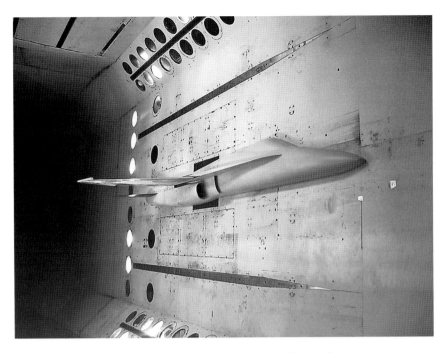

A half-span model of the F-18 was tested in Langley Research Center's Transonic Dynamics Tunnel to validate predictive methods and identify critical parameters for the flight research program. (NASA)

stabilator mounted on an interior wall of the TDT test section. Because the study called for static rather than dynamic aeroelastic tests, model designers needed to consider only the ratio between stiffness and aerodynamic loads. There was no need to duplicate the airplane's mass and inertia characteristics. The TDT was configured to allow researchers to duplicate test points planned for the full-scale flights by specifying desired combinations of Mach number and dynamic pressure. The effects of inertial and gravitational loads on the model were considered negligible.[80]

Researchers at Langley designed the model to match the stiffness distribution and load paths of the flight vehicle and to meet specified wind tunnel model strength criteria. It was 14.11 feet long with a 5.19-foot span. The wing incorporated a machined aluminum center plate with a balsa wood aerodynamic fairing bonded to the upper and lower surfaces and contoured to provide the proper airfoil shape. While fabricating the wing, the builders used an iterative analysis and design process to match the structural stiffness

---

80. Ibid.

and aeroelastic properties of the full-scale airplane via thickness contouring. Strength requirements and limited internal space availability for instrumentation rendered this method impractical for scaling the stiffness of each control surface. Leading- and trailing-edge flaps for the model were therefore constructed from stiff aluminum skins and spars. Flexible yet strong hinge-line flexures were added to compensate for stiffness but to allow the control surfaces to deform under load, mimicking the static aeroelastic qualities of the flight vehicle. The model was mounted to a turntable set into the tunnel sidewall through a five-component balance that was instrumented to measure loads. During test runs, the turntable was used to set the model's angle of attack. Technicians instrumented the wing with 80 unsteady pressure transducers, 26 strain gages, and 15 accelerometers to collect data on static pressures, torsion and bending loads, and hinge moments. An optical device called the Videogrammetric Model Deformation System measured deflection of the wing and control surfaces under aerodynamic load. In order to eliminate reflections and excessive yawing moments resulting from the model's proximity to the wall, the canted vertical tail fin was not included.[81]

Langley researchers faced the challenge of reproducing the full-scale flight vehicle's static aeroelastic characteristics in the wind tunnel model. This was accomplished through a process called wind tunnel to atmospheric mapping (WAM). Several nondimensional parameters had to be the same for both the vehicle and the model, and the two had to be tested at conditions with matching Mach numbers and identical ratios of stiffness to aerodynamic forces. Additionally, the aerodynamic pressure distribution and the stiffness distribution within the structure had to be maintained. By varying free parameters (such as Mach number and dynamic pressure) and calculating the model's dynamic pressure, researchers created a three-dimensional surface on which both the model and flight vehicle are represented so that all flight conditions map to corresponding wind tunnel conditions.[82]

Static aeroelastic research in Langley's TDT was an essential part of the AAW program. The closed-circuit variable-pressure wind tunnel is located at sea level, and it is designed to use either ordinary air or tetrafluoroethane (R134a) heavy gas as a test medium. The speed of sound at sea level pressure is 1,115 feet per second in air and 540 feet per second in R134a. The higher density and lower Mach number associated with R134a allows more latitude

---

81. Ibid.

82. Jennifer Heeg, Charles V. Spain, and J.A. Rivera, "Wind Tunnel to atmospheric Mapping for Static Aeroelastic Scaling," AIAA 2004-2044, presented at the 45th AIAA/ASME/ASCE/AHS/ASC Structures, Structural Dynamics and Materials Conference, Palm Springs, CA, April 2004.

in model construction, and the variable pressure capability allows researchers to control Mach number and dynamic pressure as needed.[83]

Wind tunnel test results confirmed some accepted ideas regarding stability and control derivatives of an aeroelastic configuration under transonic conditions. These included the increasing authority of leading-edge control surfaces and decreasing authority of trailing-edge control surfaces. Researchers also discovered unexpected behavior, including rolling moment reversal of a leading-edge control surface. Derivatives due to trailing-edge control-surface deflections tended to be gradual throughout the transonic region whereas those for leading-edge control surfaces were more pronounced. In many instances, linear analysis did not precisely predict behavior of the wind tunnel model but provided valuable insight into the physics of model design, testing, data reduction, and interpretation.[84]

F-18 Control Law Development

Hardware testing was only part of the process. A significant amount of effort went into development of control law software. In order to reduce the overall cost of the flight program, researchers approached the control laws as 18 separate point designs rather than 1 single design covering the desired range of test conditions. Boeing programmers developed these control laws using the company's Integrated Structure/Maneuver Design (ISMD) procedure; NASA Dryden engineers developed an alternate set using different software. ISMD is a computer code designed to enable structural sizing and control-surface deflections during preliminary design of a new wing. It determines the optimum control-surface deflections necessary for flexible, trimmed flight maneuver loads. Programmers at Dryden used the Control Designer's Unified Interface (CONDUIT), a software design tool that employs a multi-objective function optimization for tuning select control system design parameters. Researchers modified the CONDUIT to incorporate a nonlinear F-18 simulation for time history analysis. The primary goal was creating a controller that would maximize roll performance at 18 specified design points, using only the wing surfaces, while maintaining structural loads within design limits and providing adequate handling qualities. Load limit requirements led to development of a predictive structural loads model for use in control law design. Researchers

---

83. Ibid.

84. Heeg et al., "Experimental Results from the Active Aeroelastic Wing Wind Tunnel Test Program."

used flight data collected during Phase 1 testing to refine control laws for the Phase 2 flight-test series.[85]

The NASA team also employed MATLAB, a numerical computing environment and fourth-generation programming language that enables matrix manipulations, data plotting, and implementation of algorithms. The AAW software included a set of lateral-directional control laws to govern the airplane's roll mode and longitudinal flight control laws to control short-period motion. Because the primary design objective was to maximize aircraft roll control using only the wing, AAW control laws were programmed to command all eight wing control surfaces to aeroelastically twist the wing into optimal shapes for generating wing control power at high dynamic pressures.[86]

While designing the control laws, programmers at Boeing developed tools and guidelines for application of AAW technology. In order to ensure pilot safety, AAW flight control laws were designed to prevent the aircraft from exceeding any structural load limits encountered during normal operations or from creating adverse transients conditions during reversion to baseline flight control laws. Roll authority was attained using only the wings and associated control surfaces. The horizontal stabilators provided no roll contribution during AAW flight-test maneuvers.[87]

Baseline F-18 control laws were programmed to command the inboard and outboard leading-edge flaps as though they composed a single surface. In the RFCS mode, however, the surfaces acted independently. Researchers expected the aileron and outboard leading-edge flap to have the most significant effect on control of wing flexibility. Consequently, to exploit this characteristic, the LEFDS was programmed to increase performance of the outboard leading-edge flap through increased travel and rate. Increased actuator performance allowed programmers greater flexibility for acquiring PID data during flight-testing and for designing the AAW control laws.[88]

The AAW control laws resided within the 68040 coprocessor. They were programmed in the Ada computer language and derived from the basic production F-18 controller architecture. The lateral axis control laws provided

---

85. Ryan P. Dibley, Michael J. Allen, Robert Clarke, Joseph Gera, and John Hodgkinson, "Development and Testing of Control Laws for the Active Aeroelastic Wing Program," NASA Dryden Flight Research Center, NASA TM-2005-213666 (December 2005).

86. Pendleton, Voracek, Reichenbach, and Griffin, "The X-53: A Summary of the Active Aeroelastic Wing Flight Research Program."

87. Ibid.

88. Field et al., "The Active Aeroelastic Wing (AAW) Flight Research Program, the X-53—Final Report."

Mike Allen (left) and Thang Quatch use a simulator at Dryden to work on development of the AAW control laws. (Jim Mills)

normal bank angle and roll control. Since one of the primary research goals was to achieve roll control solely through wing surfaces, it was necessary for programmers to disestablish stabilator inputs. The longitudinal-axis control laws provided short period damping and allowed the pilot to command load factor. Directional control laws provided normal pilot control of the directional axis.[89]

---

89. Marty Brenner, William Lokos, John Carter, and David F. Voracek, "Objectives and Requirements Document—Active Aeroelastic Wing (AAW)," NASA Dryden Flight Research Center, AAW-840-ORD-v1.0 (July 1998), provided by Dave Voracek, NASA Dryden Flight Research Center, from personal files.

The AAW test bed flies formation with a production model F-18 serving as a chase plane. (NASA)

CHAPTER 2:

Phase 1 Flight Testing

In order to ensure a safe and thorough flight evaluation program, the research team divided F-18 AAW flight testing into two phases. The first consisted of parameter identification (PID) maneuvers for model validation and the second was devoted to control law development. The primary objective of Phase 1 testing was to acquire data for improved understanding of fundamental technical issues important in the validation of AAW technology. These included aerodynamics, structural characteristics, and aircraft maneuvering performance. During Phase 1, researchers developed a concept of operations for getting the modified F-18 to planned supersonic test points. This presented a challenge; the airplane's performance limitations prohibited level acceleration to the highest dynamic pressure test points, making it necessary to set up the desired Mach number at a higher altitude and then diving to the desired altitude while maintaining the Mach number. Project engineers also wanted to correlate wind tunnel data and aerodynamic performance predictions with actual flight-test data for improved simulation modeling. The aircraft was instrumented to measure roll, yaw, and pitch rates, as well as control inputs, surface deflections, and control-surface frequency response.[1]

In the initial phase of flight testing, researchers planned to experimentally characterize aircraft control effectiveness by using a software program that sent actuator commands to the AAW test bed's aerodynamic control surfaces. Special software known as an onboard excitation system (OBES) was programmed to send 31 separate maneuvers to the RFCS. Six of these maneuvers provided PID data for aeroelastic model validation. The other 25 consisted of frequency sweeps in which aircraft control surfaces were individually deflected so engineers could extract loads and validate aerodynamic control derivatives. These latter maneuvers supported an investigation of aeroservoelastic effects, as well as leading-edge-flap maneuvers and failure simulations. Researchers

---

1. Pendleton, Voracek, Reichenbach, and Griffin, "The X-53: A Summary of the Active Aeroelastic Wing Flight Research Program."

AAW phase I flight test order of operations.

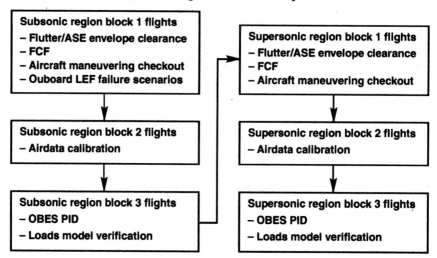

The first phase of flight research consisted of aircraft checkout and parameter identification maneuvers made to improve the understanding of fundamental technical issues necessary to validate AAW technology. (NASA)

used the OBES maneuvers to create a new aerodynamic model for the modified F-18.[2]

For safety reasons, the control laws imposed a restricted flight envelope for each OBES maneuver. This limited normal and lateral acceleration, pitch and yaw rates, and roll rate to levels that would prevent accidental overstressing of the aircraft's structure. As a result, no OBES maneuvers could be flown at two of the supersonic test points because they were outside the airplane's performance envelope. Researchers had, in fact, expected these test points to be outside the normal level-flight performance envelope, but they had hoped to achieve them in a shallow dive.[3]

Using a buildup approach, the AAW research pilot performed Integrated Test Block (ITB) maneuvers at each test point. These consisted of aeroservoelastic OBES maneuvers, aerodynamic and loads model OBES doublets, 5-g windup turns (WUTs), bank-to-bank and 360-degree rolls up to full lateral

2. Corey G. Diebler and Stephen B. Cumming, "Active Aeroelastic Wing Aerodynamic Model Development and Validation for a Modified F/A-18A Airplane," NASA TM-2005-213668 (November 2005).

3. Clarke, Allen, Dibley, Gera, and Hodgkinson, "Flight Test of the F/A-18 Active Aeroelastic Wing Airplane."

stick inputs (limited by loads), and 4-g rolling pullouts (RPOs). Push-over-pull-up (POPU) maneuvers were included for the purposes of air data calibration but were not part of the ITB. The pilot executed a POPU by pushing forward on the stick to enter a −1-g dive and then pulling back to 3 g's. An RPO required banking the airplane, pulling back on the stick to maintain a level 4-g turn, then quickly rolling the airplane 180 degrees in the opposite direction while maintaining a constant longitudinal stick position. For a WUT, the pilot banked the aircraft and pulled back on the stick, increasing acceleration while maintaining constant altitude. These maneuvers, flown using the standard F-18 control laws, provided data used to validate the new aerodynamic model. Initially, researchers planned to use only the OBES maneuvers during model development, but they discovered that analytical results did not produce a wide enough range of data. They alleviated the problem by using the POPU, RPO, and WUT data in conjunction with the OBES data in order to expand the angle-of-attack and normal acceleration ranges used in the analysis. This approach effectively eliminated discrepancies previously seen in high-g maneuvers.[4]

The aircraft was instrumented to measure time-dependent aeroelastic wing twist and bending responses as well as associated strain fields caused by aerodynamic and control forces and high-g maneuvers. Researchers also measured aircraft maneuvering response in terms of roll, yaw, and pitch rates. Measurement of control inputs, surface deflections, flight loads, and control-surface frequency response provided additional data for simulation and modeling refinement. Phase 1 flight data also provided information for evaluating control-surface effectiveness for roll control and to help researchers understand under what conditions aileron reversal occurs. Understanding all of these data were critical to designers seeking to incorporate AAW technology into flight control systems for future aircraft.[5]

A total of 50 Phase 1 flights plus one follow-on sortie were made between November 15, 2002, and June 25, 2003. These flights verified FCC software functions and the capability of the baseline F-18 control laws to fly the aircraft. Research goals accomplished included loads verification, aeroservoelastic (ASE) envelope clearance, air data calibration, PID flights, and ITB maneuvers. Engineers used ASE modeling (which takes into account structures,

---

4. Ibid.

5. Pendleton, Voracek, Reichenbach, and Griffin, "The X-53: A Summary of the Active Aeroelastic Wing Flight Research Program."

aerodynamics, sensors, mechanical actuators, and digital controls) to evaluate the feedback mechanism between structural elasticity and unsteady aerodynamics.[6]

Plans called for 30 to 40 PID flights at a rate of 3 or 4 per week. Designers at Boeing's Phantom Works used the resulting data to refine wing effectiveness models and develop the final AAW flight control software for Phase 2. Pete Flick, AAW program manager for the AFRL Air Vehicles Directorate, noted, "Acquiring the parameter identification flight data is a major step toward our ultimate goal of designing wings with AAW technology."[7]

Functional check flights (FCFs) prior to each research flight ensured the functionality of aircraft systems and instrumentation. The Phase 1 test plan was divided into three blocks and included subsonic, transonic, and supersonic test points. Block 1 objectives included FCF sorties, flutter and ASE envelope clearance, and aircraft maneuvering checkouts. One investigation included a simulated leading-edge-flap failure. Block 2 flights consisted of air data calibration sorties. Block 3 consisted of OBES PID and loads model verification.[8] Planners developed a test matrix consisting of 18 separate test points, including 9 at subsonic speeds (3 at Mach 0.85, 3 at Mach 0.9, and 3 at Mach 0.95) and 9 at supersonic speeds (4 at Mach 1.1, 3 at Mach 1.2, and 2 at Mach 1.3). Dynamic pressures during flight ranged from 600 to 1,500 psf. When setting up each test condition, the pilot relied on the production F-18 air data system, which did not have good calibration above Mach 1, and onboard Global Positioning System (GPS). Data from the research nose boom were more accurate but were not displayed to the pilot during flight.[9]

Flightcrew

Dana Purifoy and Dick Ewers served as project pilots. A former Air Force test pilot, Purifoy had previously served as a project pilot in the two joint NASA–Air Force programs at Dryden: the X-29 Forward Swept Wing and the Advanced Fighter Technology Integration F-16. After retiring from the Air Force, he returned to Dryden as a NASA research pilot in August 1994.

---

6. Levine, "Key Roles: AAW taps into Dryden's knowledge, experience and flight research savvy."

7. Alan Brown, "AAW makes first flight," *The X-Press* 44, no. 4, NASA Dryden Flight Research Center (November 2002): p. 16.

8. Pendleton, Voracek, Reichenbach, and Griffin, "The X-53: A Summary of the Active Aeroelastic Wing Flight Research Program."

9. Diebler and Cumming, "Active Aeroelastic Wing Aerodynamic Model Development and Validation for a Modified F/A-18A Airplane."

Project pilot Dana Purifoy. (NASA)   Project pilot Dick Ewers. (NASA)

During the next 11 years, he flew the NF-15B Advanced Control Technology for Integrated Vehicles test bed, F-18 Systems Research Aircraft, F-15B aeronautics research test bed, and the F-16XL Supersonic Laminar Flow Control experiment. He also piloted the NB-52B mother ship during launches of the X-38 prototype crew return vehicle and X-43A hypersonic scramjet vehicles, conducted Space Shuttle tire tests with a modified Convair 990, and worked on the X-36 tailless fighter agility project before being assigned as project pilot for the F-18 AAW.[10]

Ewers came to Dryden as a research pilot in May 1998 and flew airborne science missions in Learjet and DC-8 flying laboratories, as well as research and support missions in the F-18, King Air, and NB-52B. He had previously spent more than 8 years as an engineering test pilot with Northrop Grumman's Electronic Sensors and Systems Division (formerly Westinghouse's Electronic Systems Group), where he flight-tested emerging radar and forward-looking infrared systems under development for military and civilian use. Before joining Westinghouse, Ewers served more than 21 years in the Marine Corps as a fighter and test pilot. His military flying included combat service in Vietnam and operational exchange tours with both Navy and Air Force squadrons flying F-4s around the world, including launches from and landings on aircraft

---

10. Dana D. Purifoy, research pilot biography, NASA Dryden Flight Research Center, *http://www.nasa.gov/centers/dryden/news/Biographies/Pilots/bd-dfrc-p013.html*, September 2010, accessed July 20, 2012.

carriers.[11] He was also one of the original pilots involved in testing the pre-production F-18, primarily flying loads demonstrations. "The early F-18 had a serious problem with the wings," he recalled. "They were so flexible that the aileron essentially acted as a trim tab, twisting the wing and reducing control power. Stiffening the wings of the production airframes solved that problem, but for the AAW program we came full circle by making the wings more flexible again. It was neat because we showed that leading edge devices could be used to produce roll power."[12]

Functional Check Flight

Preparations for the maiden flight began with the ground portion of the FCF, dubbed "Flight 0," on August 7, 2002. For the purpose of developing crew coordination and performing control room procedures training, Dick Ewers sat in the cockpit, working through various checklists for OBES maneuvers and a simulated leading-edge-flap failure. He also checked out aircraft systems and control-surface functionality.[13]

The first flight occurred on November 15 with Dana Purifoy at the controls. Objectives included performing the airborne portion of the FCF, flutter clearance for two baseline test points, and outboard leading-edge-flap-failure emulation maneuvers. The purpose of evaluating the failure scenario was to verify that sufficient control power was available to fly the airplane at approach speeds with one leading-edge outboard control surface deflected upward and locked into position. The airplane lost GPS/Inertial Navigation System (INS) data and telemetry during engine startup, but Purifoy managed to restore these systems prior to takeoff. He experienced no adverse handling qualities during the 1.14-hour flight, but he noted minor asymmetric buffet on the left wing. During the flap-failure scenario, he slowed to landing speeds and increased angle of attack (AOA). Passing through approximately 10 degrees AOA at Mach 0.35, the airplane's wing stalled, causing a steep bank angle.

---

11. Richard G. Ewers, research pilot biography, NASA Dryden Flight Research Center, *http://www. nasa.gov/centers/dryden/news/Biographies/Pilots/bd-dfrc-p025.html*, February 2012, accessed July 20, 2012.

12. Richard G. Ewers, personal communication to author, December 14, 2012.

13. Leslie Welch, "Active Aeroelastic Wing (AAW) Test Report: Aircraft Functional Ground Check," August 2002, provided by Dave Voracek, NASA Dryden Flight Research Center, from personal files.

The AAW test bed takes off on its maiden flight. (NASA)

Purifoy recovered easily and was able to repeat the maneuver.[14] The AAW team was extremely happy with the results. "This first flight milestone is one we've been waiting for," Boeing Phantom Works President Bob Krieger said, "and it's only the beginning of a new chapter in the combination of aerodynamics, structures, and flight controls into a single integrated system."[15]

"This is the beginning of the twenty-first century aircraft," said Denis Bessette, "where morphing technology will create wings that bend and shape themselves for aircraft control and efficient flight from low to high speeds, and from low to high altitudes. We're expecting very productive research."[16]

---

14. David Voracek, Ed Pendleton, Eric Reichenbach, Kenneth Griffin, and Leslie Welch, "The Active Aeroelastic Wing Flight Research Program: Summary of Technical Program and Phase 1 Flight Research," presented at the RTO AVT Symposium on Novel Vehicle Concepts and Emerging Vehicle Technologies, Brussels, Belgium, April 7–10, 2003.

15. Brown, "AAW makes first flight," p. 16.

16. Ibid., p. 1.

Test maneuvers included banks and rolls at various stick deflections to evaluate the airplane's handling qualities and interaction between the wing and the control system. (NASA)

Envelope Expansion

Purifoy and Ewers took turns flying the airplane as they pressed on with the Block 1 flights. The next four sorties included aeroservoelastic envelope expansion, flutter clearance, and comparison of aircraft flying qualities using both the standard F-18 flight controls and the RFCS. Maneuvers in 18 individual test points included bank-to-bank rolls at various stick deflections, 360-degree rolls, and rolling pullouts to evaluate the airplane's handling qualities and interaction between the wing and the control system. Flutter clearance maneuvers consisted of test points with increasing dynamic pressures.[17] The last two Block 1 flights included an integrated FCF and a symmetric loads investigation. Each sortie increased the subsonic speed envelope in incremental steps from 485 knots (Mach 0.91) to 595 knots (Mach 0.98). Block 1 was completed on November 26, 2002.[18]

---

17. Voracek, Pendleton, Reichenbach, Griffin, and Welch, "The Active Aeroelastic Wing Flight Research Program: Summary of Technical Program and Phase 1 Flight Research."

18. Leslie M. Welch, "Active Aeroelastic Wing (AAW) NASA F/A-18 #853 Flight Report: Flights 1-5," NASA, November 2002, provided by Dave Voracek, NASA Dryden Flight Research Center, from personal files.

The goal of Block 2 was to calibrate the pitot-static and flow-angle measurement systems and quantify errors so the airplane's instruments would accurately measure velocity, Mach number, angle of attack, and sideslip. On December 10, each pilot flew one hour-long sortie to perform air data calibration maneuvers. Ewers reported that during acceleration to Mach 0.97, the "altimeter wound off a couple of hundred feet," indicating an altitude error.[19] During repositioning turns throughout the flight, the airplane hovered around the 45-degree angle of bank (AOB) limit, sometimes reaching up to 48 degrees AOB. Purifoy completed the air data calibration maneuvers, with some repeats. He also noted an altimeter jump at Mach 0.97 during acceleration.[20] With indicated altitude errors of up to several thousand feet in the transonic region, the AAW pilots had to fly the indicated Mach number while relying on GPS data to maintain desired altitude.[21]

Block 3 flight testing began on December 20 with more outboard leading-edge-flap-failure emulations and PID maneuvers at subsonic test conditions. The PID data were critical to the success of the AAW program because they were needed to update the existing aerodynamic database and improve the loads database, both vital to control law design.[22] Both pilots reported that the aircraft was responsive and easily controllable. Roll power was smooth at around 7.5 degrees AOA, but there was slight buffeting at about 8.1 degrees. After one flight, Purifoy suggested the pilots might need a few minutes between rolls and noted that some test points were difficult and unrepeatable, and that the aileron may have been stalling during some maneuvers.[23]

Often flying two or three sorties in a single day, Purifoy and Ewers continued to gather PID data from OBES maneuvers, integrated test blocks, and loads buildup maneuvers within the subsonic flight envelope. They performed some rolling maneuvers for comparison with earlier tests that had been made in Dryden's F-18 Systems Research Aircraft (SRA). In 1999, a series of SRA

19. Leslie M. Welch, "Active Aeroelastic Wing (AAW) NASA F/A-18 #853 Flight Report: Flights 6–7," NASA, December 2002, provided by Dave Voracek, NASA Dryden Flight Research Center, from personal files, p. 5.

20. Ibid., p. 6.

21. Clarke, Allen, Dibley, Gera, and Hodgkinson, "Flight Test of the F/A-18 Active Aeroelastic Wing Airplane."

22. Voracek, Pendleton, Reichenbach, Griffin, and Welch, "The Active Aeroelastic Wing Flight Research Program: Summary of Technical Program and Phase 1 Flight Research."

23. Leslie M. Welch, "Active Aeroelastic Wing (AAW) NASA F/A-18 #853 Flight Report: Flights 8–11," NASA, January 2003, provided by Dave Voracek, NASA Dryden Flight Research Center, from personal files, p. 6.

The AAW test bed flies upside down during a 360-degree aileron roll maneuver. (NASA)

tests had served as a precursor to the AAW flights for the purpose of collecting baseline data. For these tests, NASA technicians equipped the SRA, which had standard production F-18 wings and control surfaces, with RFCS and OBES software nearly identical to that later used on the AAW test bed, and the SRA pilot flew OBES maneuvers at each of the AAW planned test points.[24]

AAW researchers made several surprising discoveries during Phase 1 testing. First, they found that aileron hinge-moment loads frequently prevented testing full lateral-stick inputs during 1-g and elevated-g roll maneuvers in standard F-18 FCS mode. This was problematic because these maneuvers had been designed to produce baseline data for comparison with Phase 2 roll performance results, and the aileron hinge-moment problem subsequently drove development of the Phase 2 FCS software. Another surprise came when engineers noted that the aileron was subject to structural deformation at high dynamic pressures. This was due, at least in part, to the location of the aileron actuator at the far inboard edge of the control surface; the outboard edge was attached via a free hinge. The final surprise was that the control laws required much larger wing control-surface deflections to achieve adequate roll control than had been expected. In hindsight, researchers noted, "the OBES maneuvers should have exercised the leading-edge control surfaces over larger ranges to reduce the extrapolation used

---

24. Diebler and Cumming, "Active Aeroelastic Wing Aerodynamic Model Development and Validation for a Modified F/A-18A Airplane."

in the development of the aerodynamics and loads models."[25]

Supersonic PID data flights began on March 4, 2003, and Ewers reported that the airplane performed well as he accelerated to 558 knots (Mach 1.28).[26] Other Block 3 flights included supersonic flutter/ASE and loads clearance, and RFCS checkout. Ewers flew the final two Phase 1 test points on April 15, 2003. "The first phase focused on…evaluating control surface effectiveness at rolling the aircraft or testing the wing," said

AAW chief engineer Dave Voracek (left) and Dryden AAW project manager Larry Myers discuss research plans. (NASA)

Dryden AAW project manager Larry Myers. "We flew test points at altitudes ranging from 5,000 to 25,000 feet, and at speeds from Mach 0.8 to 1.3."[27]

"We've gotten excellent results," Myers added, "good agreement with our predicted results, and it looks like we've demonstrated and proven the concept."[28]

The completion of this portion of the program came almost a century after the Wright brothers made their historic flight at Kitty Hawk. Over the next few months, engineers at Dryden and Boeing would analyze the extensive collection of data and integrate it into the new RFCS control law software. Dave Voracek, chief engineer for the project, looked forward to the second test phase, in which AAW control laws would bring a modern twist to the Wright's wing-warping concept. "Phase one identified how each control surface affected the loads and dynamics of the aircraft and how it rolled and performed," he said in a 2003 interview. "Now we know how each control surface reacts, and we've designed control laws around that."[29]

---

25. Clarke, Allen, Dibley, Gera, and Hodgkinson, "Flight Test of the F/A-18 Active Aeroelastic Wing Airplane," pp. 14–15.

26. Leslie M. Welch, "Active Aeroelastic Wing (AAW) NASA F/A-18 #853 Flight Report: Flights 17–25," NASA, March 2003, provided by Dave Voracek, NASA Dryden Flight Research Center, from personal files, p. 5.

27. Jay Levine and Sarah Merlin, "Phase One: First flights set the stage for advances in AAW technology," *The X-Press*: Special Active Aeroelastic Wing Edition, NASA Dryden Flight Research Center (December 17, 2003): p. 3.

28. Alan Brown, "AAW notes from video interview," January 12, 2004, from NASA Dryden Public Affairs files provided by Alan Brown.

29. Levine and Merlin, "Phase One: First flights set the stage for advances in AAW technology," p. 3.

The modified F-18 maneuvers through a test point during the second phase of flight research. (NASA)

CHAPTER 3:

Phase 2 Flight Testing

Nearly 6 weeks after the nominal completion of Phase 1, Dana Purifoy flew a follow-on AAW research flight to address a few items that had not been covered during the initial tests. At this time, the airplane underwent inspections, maintenance, and installation of additional flight-test instrumentation. It was also prepared for static display at several air shows scheduled to take place throughout the Midwest that summer in connection with nationwide Centennial of Flight celebrations. These included the Dayton International Air Show at Dayton, OH; the Grissom Air Reserve Base air show at Kokomo, IN.; and the Experimental Aircraft Association's Air Venture 2003 at Oshkosh, WI.; as well as a fly-by of the Air Force Academy at Colorado Springs, CO, and stopovers at Whiteman Air Force Base, MO, Salina, KS, and Grand Junction, CO. Ewers and Purifoy shared flying duties during a series of eight cross-country legs spread over nearly 3 weeks.[1]

By mid-December 2004, the new software was installed and the program was ready to proceed to the second phase of flight testing. Phase 2 consisted of 34 AAW control law development flights plus 1 follow-on sortie. The primary goal was to evaluate the ability of the research flight control system software to effectively drive the AAW control surfaces for roll control at transonic and supersonic speeds. Planners helped reduce design and testing costs by treating each of the test points as a separate design point. Instead of developing a full envelope control law, programmers reduced the problem to 18 distinct design test points without interpolation between points. Each one had its own static and impact pressure envelope based on Phase 1 test data. Programmers designed control laws for each test point using the true conditions that represented the center of all of the OBES doublet maneuvers performed at that condition. The Phase 2 RFCS had the same arming and disengage envelopes as had been required for the Phase 1 maneuvers. Because the gains were locked after the system was armed and engaged, it was not required that the disengage envelope be distinct. Overlap with other test envelopes allowed the limits on

---

1. Alan Brown, "AAW wraps up first phase," *The X-Press* 45, no. 4, NASA Dryden Flight Research Center (June 27, 2003): p. 11.

The second phase of flight testing evaluated the ability of the RFCS software to effectively drive AAW control surfaces for roll control at transonic and supersonic speeds. (NASA)

the disengage envelope to compensate for the difficulty of maintaining airspeed and altitude during supersonic maneuvers.[2]

Control Law Architecture

Engineering teams at Dryden and the Boeing Phantom Works each developed a set of requirements and AAW control laws. Far from being a frivolous duplication of effort, this approach provided additional design options and ensured that all team members would have a thorough grasp of the complexities of the AAW control law design process. The Boeing team used the ISMD process and the NASA engineering team employed CONDUIT, each approach having unique strengths and weaknesses. The greatest benefit was that each method solved a slightly different, but related, design-optimization problem. The ISMD approach minimized loads while meeting roll performance constraints. The CONDUIT approach maximized the airplane's roll rate while

---

2. Clarke, Allen, Dibley, Gera, and Hodgkinson, "Flight Test of the F/A-18 Active Aeroelastic Wing Airplane," p. 15.

satisfying all other requirements as explicit constraints. ISMD results necessitated a postdesign analysis of other requirements and some additional redesign
efforts. Overall, the Boeing control law architecture was essentially the same
as that used during the TDT model tests.[3]

For the purposes of the demonstration program, the AAW control laws
had to be compatible with existing F-18 control laws while accounting for the
quasi-steady nature of ISMD-recommended gains. The ISMD-recommended
differential and collective gains were developed from sets of trimmed roll rates,
roll accelerations, normal accelerations, and pitch accelerations. Since aircraft
sensors did not provide pitch and roll accelerations, programmers developed
pseudo accelerations using command-versus-feedback errors. The directional
control law architecture was the same as that used on the baseline F-18 control
system except that the rolling-surface-to-rudder interconnect was replaced with
a roll-rate feedback path. Because the test bed aircraft was to rely solely on wing
control surfaces for rolling power, control laws for the differential stabilator
(rolling tail) were not included.[4]

NASA and Boeing engineers disagreed on which aerodynamic database
should serve as the basis for AAW control law development. NASA engineers
advocated for using the AAW database developed from Phase 1 PID data. The
Boeing team preferred the most recent production F-18 aerodynamic database,
modified by aeroelastic analyses. In the interest of moving forward while assur-
ing flight safety, both parties agreed that the AAW control laws had to be flyable
on both simulations until the issue was resolved. This resulted in the development of nine point designs based on the NASA aerodynamic data, eight point
designs based on the Boeing data, and one compromise point design, all of which
were then programmed into the RFCS software. Changing from the original 18
Boeing test points to the 9-8-1 balance necessitated a great deal of care to ensure
that code changes were performed properly and gains correctly loaded.[5]

In Phase 2, AAW project engineers correlated flight-test results with ISMD
predictions with regard to roll rate and structural loading. The ISMD method,
pioneered by Rockwell during the early AFW studies, enables simultaneous
design of control laws and aircraft structures. It may be used to determine
optimized control-surface deflections to minimize an objective function (such
as internal loads or aerodynamic drag) while simultaneously achieving desired
performance for a set of aircraft state-design variables. Although the ISMD

---

3. Ibid., p. 16.

4. Field et al., "The Active Aeroelastic Wing (AAW) Flight Research Program, the X-53—Final
Report," p. 218.

5. Ibid., p. 268.

process can be applied to optimizing control-surface deflections for an existing aircraft such as the F-18, it is best suited to use with a new aircraft design.[6]

David Riley, Boeing Phantom Works AAW project manager, explained the goal of validating design tools such as ISMD for application of AAW technology to future air vehicles. "We'd like to apply the process to a new aircraft design," he said. "We want to apply the technology early on in the design process so you can take weight out of the aircraft and make up for that through effective use of control surfaces…to give us the same performance we would have with the old approach."[7]

AAW Flight-Testing

Initial plans for Phase 2 flight-testing called for flying the Boeing-designed test points and then checking the compromise flight-test condition. Data collected during rolling maneuvers would be used to verify the accuracy of the NASA aerodynamic database developed during Phase 1. The compromise gain set, to be flown at Mach 1.2 and 20,000 feet, served as a test case for the two aerodynamic databases developed by NASA and Boeing. The planned test conditions included a trailing-edge-flap setting that NASA engineers predicted would result in an undesirable amount of sideslip. The Boeing simulation, however, predicted that this gain set would produce acceptable levels of sideslip during rolling maneuvers up to 360 degrees. The compromise test point (known as Test Point #14) would indicate which aerodynamic database was more accurate.[8]

Testing began with two flights by Dana Purifoy on December 14, 2004. The first was a functional check followed by subsonic deflection data maneuvers at 10,000 feet and 20,000 feet. The second sortie marked the beginning of the AAW control law development flights. Purifoy spent just over an hour performing RFCS reversion checks, aeroservoelastic data maneuvers, windup turns, and roll buildup maneuvers.[9]

---

6. Ibid., pp. 208–209.

7. Jay Levine, "Phase Two: Effectiveness of wing twist for roll control will be explored," *The X-Press:* Special Active Aeroelastic Wing Edition, NASA Dryden Flight Research Center (December 17, 2003): p. 12.

8. Field et al., "The Active Aeroelastic Wing (AAW) Flight Research Program, the X-53—Final Report," p. 310.

9. Ivan A. Achondo, "Active Aeroelastic Wing (AAW) NASA F/A-18 #853 Phase II Flight Report: Flights 61-67," NASA, January 2005, provided by Dave Voracek, NASA Dryden Flight Research Center, from personal files, p. 6.

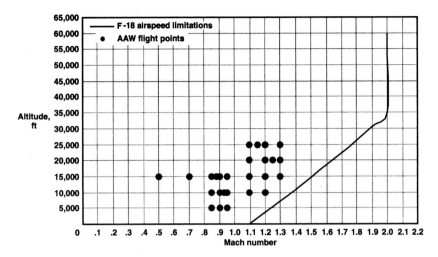

This graph illustrates the test points used to evaluate AAW control laws. (NASA)

Two more data flights were made the following day, but a postflight inspection revealed a hydraulic leak on the right main landing gear. Following several weeks of repairs, inspections, and a holiday break, flying resumed on January 5, 2005. The following day, Purifoy flew a roll buildup on Test Point #14, stopping at 60 percent stick when he noticed an indication of 2.1 degrees of sideslip. During a postflight debriefing, he commented that at Test Point #14, the aircraft demonstrated good lateral response and no longitudinal coupling. He noted that although he felt the sideslip, it was not out of the ordinary for high roll rates. On his next flight, he continued with the Test Point #14 roll buildup. He experienced no adverse handling issues, but observed that rolling with 75 percent stick input produced 3.6 degrees of sideslip and 98 percent load on the right aileron.[10]

As new control law sets were tested during the roll buildup, engineers monitored eight structural component loads for each wing against corresponding load limits. Any change to the flight control laws altered the way the aircraft generated loads, and researchers found that some control law sets encountered load limits more quickly than others. For each set of control laws, a point-to-point incremental loads clearance process had to be carried out to ensure that load limits were not exceeded. This challenging process required extraordinary teamwork between the research pilot and the engineers monitoring the load values from the control room. As the aircraft approached structural limits, the pilot was required to make very precise lateral control stick inputs, sometimes by increments of

---

10. Ibid., pp. 10-11.

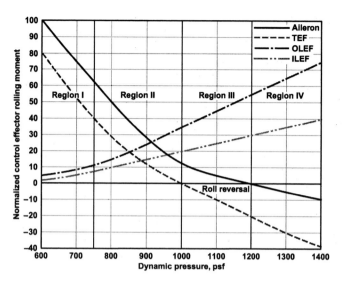

Typical roll control effectiveness of the AAW test bed is shown here as a function of dynamic pressure. (NASA)

only a few percent of the full range of motion. In order to accomplish this task, technicians installed a helpful, if unusual, research tool in the cockpit. It was affectionately referred to as the "dirty shoestring" and consisted of a short length of cord, attached with Velcro, running laterally across the cockpit just above the pilot's knees. Ink marks along its length represented incremental control stick positions, providing the pilot with a crucial visual reference. According to NASA engineer William Lokos, "It had to be re-zeroed for each flight prior to takeoff, by adjusting the string laterally after comparing the pilot's visual reference with feedback from the control room."[11] The Velcro not only allowed for easy adjustment but also prevented the cord from hindering the pilot in the event of an emergency ejection. In addition to the marked cord, AAW loads engineers developed another handy tool. A simple influence coefficient table printed on a scrap of paper was taped to one of the control room display consoles at the beginning of each flight. Using information from this table along with telemetry data measuring peak lateral stick position and maximum component loads produced by an initial maneuver, the test conductor could direct the pilot to attempt the next expansion increment without overshooting load limits. This process was successfully repeated hundreds of times. "The 'dirty shoestring' and the scrap paper look-up table did the trick," Lokos noted.[12]

---

11. William A. Lokos, personal communication to author, December 13, 2012.
12. Ibid.

Because of the dispute over the two aerodynamic databases, NASA AAW program managers had agreed to continue flying up to Test Point #14 and then brief the Flight Readiness Review (FRR) committee before continuing. It was noted that the AAW pilot was unable to complete the full-stick rolling maneuver at Mach 1.2 and 20,000 feet due to excessive sideslip and hinge-moment buildup. Since it was now clear that the NASA Dryden simulation better predicted sideslip at this flight condition, the AAW team decided to apply the ISMD process using the NASA aerodynamic data to develop three supersonic test points. NASA engineers took this opportunity to revise previous NASA test point designs, as well as those that had been designed by Boeing.[13]

Testing resumed on January 19 and continued through March. Purifoy and Ewers continued to alternate as pilots, flying ASE and roll buildup maneuvers for each of the test points. Very few significant problems occurred during the course of the program, with the exception of recurring difficulties with the leading-edge-flap drive system. The outboard leading-edge-flap asymmetry control units failed inspection and had to be repaired and retested, and the airplane was briefly grounded to repair a cracked fuselage-skin panel. While awaiting analysis of alternate control law gains, the AAW team tested a secondary control law overlay for the RFCS. NASA and Boeing engineers also created a software overlay to minimize regression testing requirements. The four final planned Phase 2 flights occurred on March 31, 2005. Each pilot flew two sorties to complete testing of the RFCS secondary control law overlay. Ewers flew a follow-on flight on April 11 to collect wing-deflection data through a flight profile at Mach 0.9 and 20,000 feet, and to perform Mach 0.85 POPU maneuvers at 10,000 and 20,000 feet.[14]

The AAW research team was extremely happy with the overall results of the program. Larry Myers summed up the 21st century twist on the Wright brothers' century-old wing-warping concept in two words: "It works!"[15]

"We have demonstrated a number of subsonic and supersonic flight conditions where we have actually taken advantage of the aeroelasticity of the wing," Myers explained. "We've gotten excellent results, good agreement with predicted results (and) roll rates are comparable to what we predicted in simulation. It looks like we've proven the AAW concept."[16]

---

13. Field et al., "The Active Aeroelastic Wing (AAW) Flight Research Program, the X-53—Final Report," p. 310.

14. Ibid., pp. 310–311.

15. Alan Brown, "AAW Phase 2 Completed," *The X-Press* 47, no. 2, NASA Dryden Flight Research Center (March 25 2005): p. 6.

16. Ibid., p. 6.

Following completion of the AAW flight research program, the F-18 test bed was redesignated the X-53 and used for a variety of projects. (NASA)

CHAPTER 4:
Follow-On Research and Future Applications

Following the successful completion of AAW flight testing, the modified F-18 assumed the role of test bed for a variety of advanced aeronautics technologies. Because of the airplane's unique configuration, Air Force officials sought to have it designated an X-plane, a vehicle solely intended for experimental flight research. This request was approved, and NASA 853 was redesignated the X-53 per memo by the Air Force Deputy Chief of Staff, Strategic Plans and Programs on August 16, 2006.1 The X-53 designation could be used retroactively, but only when referring to the aircraft as configured for AAW research. The designation no longer applied when the airplane was reconfigured as the Full-scale Advanced Systems Testbed (FAST) for later research at Dryden.

As a research workhorse, FAST would serve in several capacities. In the first, called Tier 1, it would be used as a test bed for integrating experiments that were minimally intrusive to the airplane's flight control systems. The vehicle would carry such experimental sensors, subsystems, or test fixtures. In Tier 2, it would serve as a research platform for the validation of discipline-specific or multidisciplinary, system-specific research elements requiring extensive modification of flight control systems, vehicle structure, and operation. For example, one such application would be an experiment involving adaptive flight controls. Finally, in Tier 3, the airplane would serve as a research aircraft to validate new vehicle configurations, integrated vehicle designs, and high-performance research objectives. In such cases, the airplane might need to be extensively modified.[2]

---

1. Holly Jordan, "Active Aeroelastic Wing flight research vehicle receives X-53 designation," *http://www.wpafb.af.mil/news/story.asp?id=123035661*, December 11, 2006, accessed May 20, 2012.

2. Dryden Aircraft: F/A-18 #853, *http://www.nasa.gov/centers/dryden/aircraft/F-18_853/index.html*, November 28, 2011, accessed June 18, 2012.

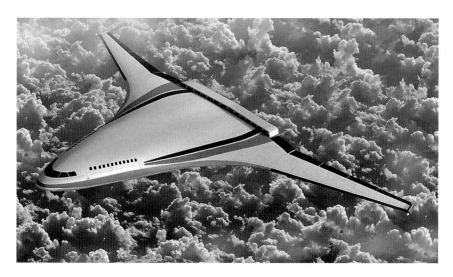

Futuristic airliner concepts such as the n3x, seen here in an artist's rendering, might include AAW technologies for optimum flying characteristics. (NASA)

The Future of AAW Technology

Although there have been no follow-on AAW flight research projects thus far, proponents of AAW technology have endeavored to promote the results of their efforts to the technical community. Since the earliest phases of AAW research, Air Force, NASA, and industry team members have published numerous technical reports and presented their findings at a variety of professional conferences.

AFRL program manager Pete Flick noted that the benefits of AAW technology depend on specific applications. Data obtained from flight testing will provide benchmark design criteria that aircraft designers can use as guidance for a wide variety of future aircraft concepts. Applications range from high-performance fighters to high-altitude/long-endurance remotely piloted and autonomous air vehicles, large transports, and high-speed/long-range aircraft. "Transitioning AAW [technology] will likely be a relatively long process since it represents a design philosophy," Flick said in a 2005 interview. "The application to future [aircraft] will depend on specific design requirements of those future systems. The benefits are greatest when a vehicle design is initiated with AAW in mind, and limited when applied to an existing vehicle."[3]

---

3. Brown, "AAW Phase 2 Completed," p. 6.

Boeing and Lockheed Martin teamed up to design this concept for a Next Generation Bomber. Such a design would be an ideal application of AAW technology. (Boeing/Lockheed Martin)

In a 1999 presentation to the North Atlantic Treaty Organization (NATO) Research and Technology Organization's Applied Vehicle Technology Panel, Flick and Michael Love of Lockheed Martin Tactical Aircraft Systems described the need for early application of AAW design features when developing future aircraft. In order to fully realize the benefits of these features, aircraft designers must account for aeroelastic effects from the beginning of the design process. The decision to apply AAW features to an aircraft will influence conceptual design decisions regarding airfoil thickness-to-chord ratio, aspect ratio, and wing torque-box geometry. Flick and Love noted that although AAW technology is being matured through flight testing, "transition of the technology to future systems will require educating designers in multiple disciplines on this new design approach."[4]

The AAW concept represents a revolutionary shift in aircraft design methods and is more multidisciplinary than conventional methods. With AAW, designers must account for interactions between flexibility effects and aerodynamics, controls, loads, and structure. The conventional approach to conceptual aircraft design constrains the design space to avoid effects such as static

---

4. Peter M. Flick and Michael H. Love, "The Impact of Active Aeroelastic Wing Technology on Conceptual Aircraft Design," *Structural Aspects of Flexible Aircraft Control*, RTO-MP-036, NATO Research and Technology Organization, presented at the Specialist's Meeting of the RTO Applied Vehicle Technology Panel, Ottawa, Canada, October 1999, p. 10-1.

Boeing is studying blended-wing-body concepts for application to new passenger/cargo transport and aerial tanker designs. (Boeing)

aeroelasticity (typically considered a disadvantage) as the design progresses. Under a new model incorporating AAW technology, designers are free to consider configurations outside the conventional design space where aeroelastic deformation provides a net advantage. Studies indicate that AAW-based designs may enable configurations with thinner and/or higher-aspect-ratio wings, and the reduction or elimination of horizontal tail surfaces. "In order to effectively exploit AAW technology," according to Flick and Love, "designers will need benchmark design studies to reference, and a design process that enables the quantification of flexibility effects on aerodynamics, control performance, loads, and structural weight."[5]

Industry interest in AAW technology has been sporadic. According to Ed Pendleton, Boeing's Gerry Miller (who had previously helped develop

---

5. Ibid., 10-4.

AFW for Rockwell) had several discussions with representatives of the company's Commercial Airplanes business unit in which he focused on trying to implement AAW on existing Boeing transports as well as on the proposed High-Speed Civil Transport (HSCT)—a Mach 2.4–capable, economically viable, supersonic-cruise airliner concept. "AAW is an enabling technology for an SST [supersonic transport]/HSCT concept," Pendleton said. "Unfortunately, Boeing canceled the HSCT effort in 1999 due to excessive development costs."[6]

Possibilities for Boeing's applications of the new aeroelastic technology suffered another setback when Scott Zillmer, the company's lead engineer for new concepts using AAW, passed away. "Scott's untimely death during the flight test part of the AAW program prevented him from turning out more concepts that took advantage of AAW," Pendleton noted. "There are benefits to applying AAW to fast heavy transports like the C-17 or Blended Wing Body aircraft."[7]

Meanwhile, the Air Force has expressed interest in applying the AAW concept to current and future high-speed combat aircraft. The most visible effort to develop future air-dominance fighters, known as the Efficient Supersonic Air Vehicle (ESAVE) program, is an ongoing set of design studies involving airframe contractors using multidisciplinary design-optimization processes to solve specific problems. The ESAVE approach is ideal for capturing discipline interactions required for implementation of active-structures technologies like AAW. Therefore, AFRL has sponsored ESAVE design efforts by Lockheed Martin to examine future high-speed fighter concepts and apply AAW technology to those designs. Just as with the early AFW studies, ESAVE project plans call for wind tunnel model tests in Langley's TDT. "There has been quite a bit of interest in our AAW flight-test results and how the leading edges on the F-18 were used," said Pendleton.[8]

As applied to ESAVE, use of AAW technology could potentially reduce wing weight, as has been demonstrated in earlier studies. Since future advanced technology aircraft configurations exceed the bounds of historical mass properties databases, designers must use a physics-based analytical approach such as a finite element model to determine realistic airframe-weight sensitivities with respect to design variables. AAW features are modeled by removing wing stiffness requirements for high-speed roll cases and optimizing control-surface schedules to minimize wing-root bending while satisfying trim requirements.

---

6. Ed Pendleton, personal communication to author, August 30, 2012.

7. Ibid.

8. Ibid.

This Boeing advanced fighter concept closely resembles a configuration examined under the Efficient Supersonic Air Vehicle (ESAVE) study. (Boeing)

Designers use the calibrated weight of finite element models to develop response-surface equations for the technology being assessed.[9]

According to Pete Flick, AFRL efforts to promote the use of AAW technology through research and application studies such as ESAVE are an important step. Through these additional research efforts, he said, "We are making progress in transitioning AAW technology to industry. It is really a change in the way we design aircraft, which is a difficult leap to make. Such a leap will benefit from a change in the design process, and AFRL has used AAW as motivation for some of our multi-disciplinary design methods research. The ESAVE program is just one example."[10]

9. Clifton Davies, Marc Stelmack, Scott Zink, Antonio De La Garza, and Pete Flick, "High Fidelity MDO Process Development and Application to Fighter Strike Conceptual design," AIAA-2012-5490, 12th AIAA Aviation Technology, Integration, and Operations Conference, Indianapolis, IN (September 2012).

10. Pete Flick, personal communication to author, August 31, 2012.

Team members from the Air Force, NASA, and Boeing contributed to the success of the AAW flight research program. (NASA)

CHAPTER 5:
Program Management and Direction

The F-18 AAW research team included participation by personnel from NASA, the Department of Defense (Air Force and Navy), industry, and academia. Their synergistic efforts assured fulfillment of all technical, management, and product transition requirements for the project.

NASA Dryden served as the responsible test organization and management lead for the flight-test program, and it provided support to Rockwell (later Boeing, following a 1996 merger) for development of detailed AFW/AAW flight control laws. Dryden also served as technical lead on aircraft systems, analytical model development, simulation, testing, and data reduction. Technicians at Dryden installed the wings and instrumentation. Larry Myers served as NASA AAW project manager, with Denis Bessette as flight research program manager and David Voracek as AAW chief engineer. With previous AFW wind tunnel experience, researchers at NASA Langley provided additional support for development of analytical models.[1]

The Air Force Research Laboratory, which had absorbed AFWL in 1997, was responsible for overall program direction, integration of participating organization objectives, integration of technologies into the flight vehicle research design, hardware procurement, analysis of resulting data for military applications, and documentation of results applicable to current and future aircraft weapon system development. The flight-test program began with the request by Lt. Col. Ken Griffin (chief of the Structures Division in AFRL's Air Vehicle Directorate) of Edmund W. Pendleton to gather the information developed by both NASA and AFRL research programs with Rockwell and explore the possibility of a flight-test program to further mature AAW technology. The resulting program was managed by AFRL and funded through a contract with Boeing and a memorandum of agreement with NASA. Pendleton served as AFRL program manager from 1992 to 2001 and as AFRL chief engineer for the AAW program from 2002 to 2005. Pete Flick served as chief engineer from 1997 to 2001

---

1. White, "Active Flexible Wing Technology Demonstration."

Dryden AAW project manager Denis Bessette. (NASA)

and as program manager from 2001 to 2005.[2] The Southwest Research Institute of San Antonio, TX, provided consulting services to AFRL under an Air Force contract. The AFFTC served as a participating test organization (PTO), assisting Dryden planners with developing flight test maneuvers required to achieve joint test objectives and in the conduct of the program and reporting of results.[3] The Naval Air Weapons Center provided F-18 data for analytical models and monitored project results for technology transition to future military systems.[4]

Boeing's Phantom Works organization designed and fabricated the wings and developed the flight control computers and software. Boeing program managers included Peter Field (August 1996–August 1998 and September 2003–March 2005), James Guffey (September 1998–April 2003), and David Riley (April 2003–September 2003). Boeing's newly acquired North American Aircraft Division (formerly Rockwell) developed the digital flight controller and supported NASA with aircraft systems, simulation, and testing. Boeing subcontracted BAE Control Systems (later, BAE Systems) to assist with modification of the F-18's computer systems and with Moog Aircraft Group to develop flight control actuators.[5]

Multi-Agency Team Building

The flight research program was the culmination of grassroots efforts by aeroelasticians in industry, NASA, and the Air Force to develop working-level interest in AFW/AAW technology. Early research collaboration between AFWL and NASA Langley laid the foundation, but no single aeroelastic research group in any single Government agency had the resources to mount a full-scale

---

2. Field et al., "The Active Aeroelastic Wing (AAW) Flight Research Program, the X-53—Final Report."

3. Kenneth J. Szalai, George K. Richey, and James P. Brady, "DRAFT—Active Aeroelastic Wing (AAW) Program Annex to the Memorandum of Understanding Between USAF Wright Laboratory (WL), Air Force Flight Test Center (AFFTC), and NASA Dryden Flight Research Center (NASA/DFRC)," January 9, 1996, provided by Dave Voracek, NASA Dryden Flight Research Center, from personal files.

4. White, "Active Flexible Wing Technology Demonstration."

5. Field et al., "The Active Aeroelastic Wing (AAW) Flight Research Program, the X-53—Final Report," p. 11.

flight-test program for AAW. Ultimately, AFRL, NASA, and Boeing had to unite their resources. Advocates fostered technical interest and highlighted the technology's value to the aerospace industry and military services. Study contracts generated industry support from companies that might otherwise have adopted a "Not Invented Here" attitude.[6]

Support for the AAW program resulted from several factors. Aircraft suitability studies with the X-31, F-16, and F-18 provided a general concept for a test bed vehicle configuration and an outline for the flight-test series. The idea of using Edwards Air Force Base and Dryden—with their combination of assets and unique resources—as the test location convinced AFRL leadership that it should sponsor the program. Researchers within the NASA aeroelastic flight-test community joined with Air Force and industry advocates to solicit NASA support. Early on, key people within AFRL recommended a joint effort with NASA because of Dryden's previous experience with innovative flight experiments and state-of-the-art flight research support facilities. Advocates such as Ed Pendleton worked to convince AFRL leadership that the multidisciplinary character of AAW technology was ideal for a joint program.[7]

AAW advocates also sought participation from the Air Force Flight Test Center at Edwards, not just to take advantage of the organization's expertise but also to preempt any detractors who felt that AFFTC should lead the effort. Ed Pendleton noted that the AFFTC, with more than half a century of flight-test experience and numerous aeronautical milestones to its credit, is first and foremost in the minds of Air Force leadership when it comes to executing innovative test projects. So, why not go to AFFTC first? "In our case," Pendleton said, "the answer was that we wanted to do both demonstration of the AAW technology and research into how the aerodynamics, flight controls, and structure all worked together to improve rolling performance on a full scale aircraft."[8]

Because Dryden specializes in flight research, it was the obvious choice to serve as the responsible test organization. This was especially obvious once the NASA F-18 had been selected as a test bed. Dryden already had significant experience with using the F-18 in a variety of comparable research efforts, including the HARV and the SRA. Additionally, Dryden and AFFTC had already established an alliance agreement to facilitate sharing of assets that included the runways and test ranges at Edwards, so adding the Air Force organization to the team made sense and circumvented rivalry. "By inviting AFFTC to join us as a

---

6. Anderson et al., "Summary of Lessons Learned from the Active Aeroelastic Wing Flight Research Program."

7. Ibid.

8. Ed Pendleton, personal communication with author, July 11, 2012.

Senior members of the Air Force team included (from left) Dr. Don Paul, chief scientist of the AFRL Air Vehicles Directorate; Edmund W. Pendleton, AFRL program manager for AAW; and AFRL commander Maj. Gen. Paul D. Nielsen. (U.S. Air Force)

team member," said Pendleton, "we defused any competitive issues that AFFTC might have harbored."[9]

The disparate agencies built a joint test team through a combination of contractor and Government advocacy and personal networking. The strongest NASA proponents at Dryden included aerodynamicists and flight controls engineers. Additional support came from NASA Langley, where researchers realized the potential value of combining the flight-test data with aeroelastic stability and control-derivative model data from wind tunnel studies. Efforts to build the contractor portion of the team were complicated by consolidation of several major aerospace companies. Lockheed had expressed interest in developing the leading-edge control surfaces, but it did not have a host aircraft that was cost competitive with the McDonnell Douglas–Rockwell team. In December 1996, Boeing merged with Rockwell's aerospace and defense units, uniting the two companies under the Boeing name. Rockwell's space systems division, aircraft division, Rocketdyne, Autonetics, missile systems, and aircraft-modification division were renamed Boeing North American and operated as a Boeing subsidiary. In August 1997, Boeing merged with McDonnell Douglas and its Phantom Works organization. Once the dust settled, the Phantom Works was assigned to head up the AAW modification effort with support from Boeing North American. Years of preparation including contractor development, analytical studies, and wind tunnel testing, as well as the relationships developed during these preliminary research efforts, helped forge a successful team.[10]

Integrated Product-Development Team Approach

NASA and industry participants formed two integrated product-development teams (IPTs) to achieve the major technical tasks. One team was responsible

---

9. Ibid.

10. Anderson et al., "Summary of Lessons Learned from the Active Aeroelastic Wing Flight Research Program."

for air-vehicle systems and flight testing, and the other for control law methods and development. NASA Dryden led the air-vehicle systems team, with support from Boeing, and was responsible for aircraft modifications, control system flight qualification, database development, simulation, and flight testing. Boeing led the control law development team with support from Dryden and Langley, and with the Southwest Research Institute and AFRL providing consultation. Both teams worked together to ensure compatibility of the control laws with the aircraft systems and to flight-qualify the integrated systems and software.[11]

The AAW program managers developed an IPT charter to define the mission statement, organization, performance goals, end product, and ground rules necessary for achieving success. This charter clarified the overall program goals, resources required from the funding organizations, and exit strategy. Further, it committed the organization—to the extent possible—to meeting program resource requirements.[12] The Air Force portion of the IPT charter described support needed from the various AFRL technical divisions responsible for aerodynamics, structures, and flight controls. During the AFW wind tunnel studies at Langley, all three divisions provided support, but during the AAW flight-test program, the flight controls group never implemented the IPT charter, and there were only two or three AFRL technical personnel on the project. According to Ed Pendleton, "There was almost no support from the Air Force flight controls group once the contract got going in late 1996 until we completed the effort in 2005. Back during wind tunnel model testing at the TDT, we enjoyed support from all three divisions, but by 1996, times had changed."[13]

The IPT integrated cost, schedule, and performance factors associated with the AAW flight-test program. NASA drove the overall project schedule, adding some tasks beyond those included in Boeing's contract with the Air Force. NASA paid the cost of these added requirements and picked up the additional workload when cost increases prevented delivery on the original Air Force contract. Mutual trust and schedule flexibility between Air Force, NASA, and Boeing program managers was crucial to success.[14]

---

11. White, "Active Flexible Wing Technology Demonstration."

12. Anderson et al., "Summary of Lessons Learned from the Active Aeroelastic Wing Flight Research Program."

13. Ed Pendleton, personal communication with author, July 10, 2012.

14. Anderson et al., "Summary of Lessons Learned from the Active Aeroelastic Wing Flight Research Program."

With landing gear and flaps down, NASA Dryden's Active Aeroelastic Wing F/A-18A research aircraft rolls toward final approach to the Edwards Air Force Base runway at the end of a test flight. (NASA)

CHAPTER 6:

Research Results and Lessons Learned

The F-18 AAW flight research program validated an air-vehicle concept in which use of a lighter, more flexible wing improved overall aircraft performance. Early design studies employing AAW techniques were applied to several fighter concepts and demonstrated the potential to reduce aircraft takeoff gross weight by as much as 5 to 20 percent. During the course of several wind tunnel test programs conducted from 1984 to 1993, AAW technology was shown to provide substantially increased control power across an aircraft's performance envelope while twisting the wing into shapes that minimized drag, reduced structural loads, and provided control for roll and pitch. The joint Air Force–NASA-industry flight research program, initiated in 1996, demonstrated AAW technology using a full-scale aircraft. The modified F-18 test bed aircraft was an ideal choice for the demonstration because of its high-speed flight capabilities and thin, flexible wings with multiple control surfaces.[1]

Overall, the flight research effort was highly successful, and it provided a safe and thorough evaluation of AAW technology. Researchers demonstrated that it was possible to exploit aeroelastic effects to improve aircraft roll performance. Data from wind tunnel and flight testing indicates that AAW technology may be applied to future aircraft designs employing thinner, lighter wings with a higher aspect ratio than possible with more conventional technology. Researchers successfully achieved all major objectives set forth in the AAW test plan.[2]

Test Bed Development

The first objective was the development of an effective full-scale test bed for exploration of AAW technology. Modification of the F-18 produced a flight-test

---

1. Ibid.
2. Pendleton, Voracek, Reichenbach, and Griffin, "The X-53: A Summary of the Active Aeroelastic Wing Flight Research Program."

article that met the requirements of the AAW investigation and increased high-speed roll control power of the outboard leading-edge flaps by 30 percent while meeting demanding load, rate, and safety requirements. An extensive research instrumentation system included more than 1,600 separate measurements that allowed for safety-of-flight monitoring, as well as establishing a database quantifying AAW technology benefits.[3] Development of the new outboard leading-edge-flap actuator resulted in four independent control surfaces per wing for improved maneuver performance and load control. The test bed's dual flight control computers and reversion capability provided sufficient safety margins for high-speed flight testing.[4] Wing modifications successfully restored stiffness levels to pre-Roll-Mod conditions, but two problems were encountered. First, more refurbishment was required than had been anticipated due to the degraded state of the existing structure. Second, the task of duplicating an obsolete structural condition was complicated by the loss of documentation and first-hand knowledge over the intervening 20 years between construction of the preproduction F-18 and the AAW wing. Electrical- and hydraulic-system modifications were completed without difficulty. Computer modeling and rapid prototyping of the new actuator facilitated design, construction, and installation of new components.[5]

Control Law Development

The second objective, development of AAW flight control laws, successfully demonstrated control-surface gearing functions used to achieve desired maneuver dynamics while controlling wing structural loads. Researchers combined analysis and modeling with test results to generate the aerodynamic and loads databases required for creating control-surface gearing functions with ISMD. The effect of AAW wing structural modifications on aerodynamic stability and control was estimated using aeroelastic analysis. The results of PID flight testing provided full-scale data for use in structural load models. Researchers combined aerodynamic and structural loads data to develop linear models. They then used the ISMD tool to create gearing functions to achieve desired combinations of maneuver dynamics and wing loads. All software was verified and validated

---

3. Ibid.

4. Field et al., "The Active Aeroelastic Wing (AAW) Flight Research Program, the X-53—Final Report," p. 323.

5. Ibid., pp. 326–327.

(V&V) to ensure flightworthiness.[6] The V&V process at Boeing's Phantom Works evolved over the course of the program and became more refined with the addition of autocoded software for the control laws. NASA helped fund the V&V effort for the addition of PID software, performed overlay upgrades, tested changes, and performed a failure effects analysis prior to flight testing. In all cases, the AAW software performed as designed.[7]

Full-Scale Demonstration

The third objective, demonstrating AAW technology with a full-scale airplane, provided accurate flight-test data to validate predictive models without compromising safety. Initial flights gave pilots an opportunity to perform basic functional checks, clear the performance envelope, calibrate air data, verify flight computer reversion capability, and verify that leading-edge-flap failure would not pose a safety hazard. Research pilots performed windup turns, rolls, and rolling pullouts to identify the operational value of AAW technology at specified flight conditions. Additional maneuvers demonstrated flight at high dynamic pressures without using the differential stabilator that augments roll power on the standard F-18. All test maneuvers were performed without exceeding structural load limits or experiencing software errors. An incremental buildup approach to flight-test procedures allowed researchers to identify potential danger and adjust AAW control laws accordingly. Tests of the full-scale AAW test bed proved that the AAW wing warping technique met the control power and handling requirements of high-performance aircraft.[8]

Evaluation of Results

Finally, the fourth objective involved collection of full-scale experimental data to improve modeling of basic nonlinear elements of the mechanics of flight and to develop an extensive database for use by researchers from the Air Force, NASA, U.S. industry, and academic institutions.[9] Evaluation of AAW flight-test results with respect to predictions and simulation identified further per-

---

6. Ibid., p. 323.

7. Ibid., p. 328.

8. Ibid., pp. 323–324.

9. Pendleton, Voracek, Reichenbach, and Griffin, "The X-53: A Summary of the Active Aeroelastic Wing Flight Research Program."

formance improvements that could have been made with additional program resources, as well as design challenges to be addressed in the application of AAW technology to future aircraft. Researchers faced their most significant challenge in developing aerodynamic and loads data that accurately captured aeroelastic effects in all axes. The availability of higher-fidelity aeroelastic analysis tools would have expedited progress. Existing models did not always sufficiently approximate the desired roll acceleration feedback, resulting in compromised effectiveness of the rolling surface-to-rudder interconnect. Although the experimental flight controls were successful in harnessing aeroelastic control power to achieve desired maneuver performance within acceptable load parameters, some limitations were imposed due to constraints associated with the production F-18 control laws. Most notably, since no roll acceleration feedback was available, it had to be approximated by differencing the commanded and actual roll rate values. Nevertheless, despite the near absence of any fine-tuning of the control laws, demonstrated AAW performance levels were quite impressive.[10]

Modeling and Predictions

Analytical modeling and ground testing served as a foundation for the AAW flight research effort. Several key disciplines were critical to the design and development of AAW modifications for the test aircraft. These included aerodynamics, aeroelastics, and loads.

Somewhat surprisingly, in retrospect, the importance of aerodynamics was underestimated because NASA and Boeing engineers did not expect that the AAW modifications would significantly alter the established aerodynamic qualities of the F-18. As the project progressed, it became apparent that a small change in wing stiffness resulted in significant aerodynamic changes. In their final analysis of the flight-test program, team members noted that "… the importance of a validated nonlinear aerodynamic database for control law design on a highly maneuverable aircraft cannot be overestimated."[11]

Throughout the course of the program, researchers used aeroelastic analyses to develop and modify flight-simulation databases. It soon became clear that linear aerodynamic methods limited the accuracy of these analyses. The AAW team felt, therefore, that analytical reliability could be improved using aerodynamic influence-coefficient correction techniques and additional wind

---

10. Field et al., "The Active Aeroelastic Wing (AAW) Flight Research Program, the X-53—Final Report," pp. 325–328.

11. Ibid., p. 327.

tunnel pressure data. Simulations were improved using flight data based on the PID results plus nonlinear maneuver updates.[12]

Loads engineers were challenged to develop accurate structural loads predictions since no good starting point was available and because the AAW flight demonstration was designed to achieve design-limit loads. The research team concluded that, "Even with the linear derivative models based on parameter identification results, correlation with flight test results is fair, underscoring the importance of developing a validated flight simulation nonlinear loads database."[13]

Ground testing in the Dryden Loads Lab allowed researchers to successfully characterize wing flexibility and the effects of AAW modifications to the F-18. Engineers used the results to establish data for correlation with the finite element model. Calibration of flight-loads instrumentation produced data for development of accurate load equations as required for reliable safety-of-flight monitoring. Ground vibration tests identified the aircraft's modal characteristics, and the structural mode interaction test demonstrated the airplane's servoelastic stability.

Costs and Benefits

Joint funding for the AAW Flight Research Program was estimated at $45 million over 10 years. Actual costs are based on value of the dollar over the calendar years (CY) 1996 through CY 2004. Costs of converting a standard F-18 into the AAW test bed included all design and hardware modifications to the wings, control surfaces, and computers, as well as development of control laws and associated software and their verification and validation. Costs associated with the flight research program included ground testing and data-gathering and reduction efforts resulting from flight research.[14]

The designers and builders of high-performance military and civil aircraft will be among the first to benefit from AAW technology, which can be applied to future high-performance aircraft operating in a broad range of subsonic, transonic, and supersonic flight conditions. Aircraft designers can use AAW technology to increase control power, reduce aerodynamic drag and airframe structural weight, and expand the design space with respect to wingspan,

---

12. Ibid., p. 327.

13. Ibid., p. 328.

14. Anderson et al., "Summary of Lessons Learned from the Active Aeroelastic Wing Flight Research Program."

leading-edge sweep, and airfoil thickness. Depending on mission requirements, these improvements should significantly reduce takeoff gross weight and overall production costs. By applying the results of this revolutionary research, aircraft manufacturers can offer affordable and competitive new air vehicles to commercial and Government customers.[15]

Designers of civil and military transport aircraft will be able to increase wing aspect ratio and/or sweep with minimal increase in structural weight. In some cases, it may be possible to decrease airfoil thickness. These features should significantly improve cruise performance and reduce fuel consumption, making aircraft more affordable to manufacture and operate. Future military fighter planes with AAW technology will have increased maneuverability at high speeds without the need for a rolling tail or stiff wing. With reduced structural weight, and potentially increased wing aspect ratio and/or sweep, these aircraft will benefit from increased range and maneuverability. At the conclusion of the early AFW wind tunnel studies, Air Force researchers declared this technology ready for flight testing. With the successful achievement of the F-18 AAW flight demonstration, the technology need only be matured for use in future designs to reduce development risk.[16]

Lessons Learned

The F-18 AAW demonstration program yielded many valuable lessons. These are applicable to a variety of disciplines including test bed suitability and modification, ground and flight testing, and program management and organization.[17]

---

15. Ibid.

16. White, "Active Flexible Wing Technology Demonstration."

17. Anderson et al., "Summary of Lessons Learned from the Active Aeroelastic Wing Flight Research Program."

1: Test Bed Suitability

Item 1-1
F-16 Design Study.

Goals
Conduct a contractor design study to explore the suitability of using a modified F-16 supersonic aircraft as an AAW technology demonstrator.

Results
A study by Lockheed Martin showed the viability of adding a leading-edge outboard control surface to the F-16 and reducing wing stiffness to improve suitability for achieving aileron reversal. The cost of modifications was estimated at approximately $30 million.

Lessons Learned
1. Use of the F-16 was a viable option, but industrial funding of program activities at the Air Force Flight Test Center would have added substantial undetermined flight-test costs.
2. Industrial funding is a substantial barrier to entry.

Item 1-2
X-31 Design Study.

Goals
Conduct a contractor design study to explore the suitability of using one of two X-31 supersonic research aircraft as an AAW technology demonstrator.

Results
This approach was abandoned following the crash of an X-31 at Edwards in 1995. The airplane was completing its final flight and would have been available for the AAW program.

Lessons Learned
When a two-of-a-kind asset is reduced to one, future use of the surviving asset becomes severely restricted. The remaining X-31 had already been allocated for use in another research project and was not available for the AAW program.

Item 1-3
F-18 Design Study.

Goals
Conduct a contractor design study to explore the suitability of using a modified F-18 supersonic aircraft as an AAW technology demonstrator.

Results
A McDonnell Douglas F-18 study demonstrated the viability of adding an actuation system to separately drive leading edge outboard flaps as AAW control surfaces. Wings manufactured for the preproduction F-18 prototypes had stiffness levels suitable for the AAW demonstration. Cost of all modifications was estimated at approximately $8 million. Boeing acquired McDonnell Douglas through a 1997 merger prior to the full-scale AAW flight demonstration program.

Lessons Learned
1. AAW flight testing ultimately proved the feasibility of the early design studies.
2. Overall F-18 AAW modification costs on an Air Force contract were $9.282 million. This number reflects Boeing modification costs but not ground or flight costs. Additional NASA costs resulted from completion of wing hydraulic plumbing and instrumentation.
3. The early studies yielded only very rough cost estimates.

Item 1-4

The application of AAW technology is important in all aerodynamic flight regimes (subsonic, transonic, and supersonic).

Goals

Demonstrate AAW capabilities at subsonic, transonic, and supersonic speeds.

Results

The research team successfully demonstrated AAW capabilities in all flight regimes.

Lessons Learned

AAW technology worked satisfactorily on the F-18 test bed, but it could be more effectively applied in a new aircraft design that incorporates AAW features.

Item 1-5

Assembling an Active Aeroelastic Wing designed for strength and freedom from buckling and flutter, with no added structural material for roll effectiveness.

Goals

Modify the wings of a supersonic aircraft to achieve AAW stiffness/structural requirements.

Results

Technicians modified the wings of a production F-18 to a stiffness level suitable for the AAW technology demonstration. Wings from one of the original preproduction F-18 prototypes were used as a starting point because they had greater flexibility than production wings.

Lessons Learned

1. The AAW design approach can be used to achieve roll performance goals without increasing wing stiffness.
2. AAW technology can be successfully applied to fighter-type aircraft with an aspect ratio of 3.5 or greater.

Item 1-6
Use of multiple leading- and trailing-edge control surfaces to exploit AAW characteristics.

Goals
Develop an aircraft wing with multiple leading- and trailing-edge control surfaces for use over a wide range of Mach numbers and dynamic pressure values.

Results
The research team developed an AAW wing for the F-18 by modifying the leading-edge-flap actuation system. Flight-test results validated the use of all control surfaces over the planned range of Mach numbers and dynamic pressures.

Lessons Learned
1. The modified leading edges on the test bed were effective at supersonic speeds but less so in the transonic range. The trailing-edge outboard surfaces were ineffective for maneuvering control at high speeds, but they were very effective for controlling structural loads.
2. Use of combinations of leading- and trailing-edge surfaces provided substantial control power and aeroelastic roll effectiveness over the demonstrated Mach and dynamic-pressure range.

Item 1-7
Use of aileron effectiveness for roll control.

Goals
Achieve aileron reversal and use reversed forces to help roll the aircraft. Early studies suggested that this goal was practical.

Results
Full aileron reversal could not be attained at achievable flight conditions with this flight-test vehicle.

Lessons Learned
Researchers expected to see aileron reversal, but aileron control power went to zero and no further.

2: Test Bed Modification

Item 2-1
Wing structural modifications for AAW demonstration.

Goals
Remove the aft solid-composite wing box covers and replace them with prepro-duction design-type honeycomb covers. The estimated cost was $2.36 million.

Results
Replaced the wing box covers at an actual cost of $2.44 million.

Lessons Learned
1. The modification, including refurbishment of wing-cover fastener holes (elongated following years of flight) to original specifications, was easily accomplished.
2. Actual costs exceeded estimates due to increased bulk charges from the Boeing shop floor.
3. Always expect surprises when refurbishing old hardware to demonstrate a new concept.

Item 2-2
Actuation of the inboard and outboard leading-edge flap drive system (LEFDS).

Goals
Segment the inboard LEFDS from outboard leading-edge flaps. Drive the outboard LEFDS by adding a new power unit, asymmetric control unit, brake, and shaft. The estimated subcontract cost was $1.4 million.

Results
Modified the LEFDS as desired and added a new power drive unit, asymmetric control unit, brake, and shaft. The actual cost was $1.56 million. The sub-contractor (Moog) funded additional quality testing after expenses exceeded contract dollars.

Lessons Learned
1. Leading-edge outboard (LEO) surfaces can be used as maneuver/ load control surfaces.
2. The new LEFDS worked well, with actuator response rates near 45 degrees per second.
3. LEO divergence was well above flight envelope for an F-18.

Item 2-3
Leading-edge inboard/outboard drive system spares.

Goals
The AAW team planned to procure one ship set of leading-edge outboard actuators and asymmetry control units (ACUs), plus a quality-test actuator as a backup.

Results
Actuator quantity proved sufficient, but brake pads on inboard and outboard ACUs drifted out of specifications.

Lessons Learned
Obtain at least one spare unit of each unique piece of hardware to avoid significant schedule delays.

Item 2-4
Flight computer.

Goals
Modify existing analog-to-digital (A/D) printed circuitboard to drive LEFDS power-distribution unit, and modify software in existing quad-redundant flight control computer. Estimated subcontractor costs were approximately $576,000.

Results
The existing board contained an excessive number of jumper modifications. The team installed a new A/D board in the FCC and made wiring changes to the chassis. Actual subcontract costs were $1.012 million.

Lessons Learned
It is important to accurately track previous software and hardware configuration changes. Previous changes affected new changes to the FCC with the subcontractor.

Item 2-5
Flight control computer spares.

Goals
The original plan was to modify only one ship set of flight control computers.

Results
NASA funded an additional FCC ship set for use in the AAW test bed.

Lessons Learned
Two ship sets are the absolute minimum required when conducting testing at two different locations even if sequential testing has been scheduled. Multiple ship sets at each location allow testing to continue in the event of unforeseen contingencies.

Item 2-6
Developing confidence in using the Integrated Structure/Maneuver Design (ISMD) Optimization Design Tool software.

Goals
Boeing planned to use ISMD, a new design tool, as a guide to develop control laws for AAW.

Results
AAW control laws were successfully demonstrated at nine transonic and nine supersonic test points.

Lessons Learned
1. ISMD gains, designed with Boeing V-Dev (F-18 project database) linear aero-software, gave designed maneuvering performance and good flying qualities in the modular 6-degrees-of-freedom (MODSDF) nonlinear piloted simulation using V-Dev nonlinear aero, with minor gain adjustments after batch nonlinear simulation. This aircraft did not need ISMD gain adjustment as a result of rigid-body stability analysis. The stability analysis used the linear design aero as the bare airframe linear analysis model.
2. The team developed confidence in the ISMD tool. Linear aero gives good results. Flying in real aero may require tweaks.
3. The MATLAB optimization function used in this study needs further improvement regarding global optimization.

Item 2-7
AAW flight control law design.

Goals

1. Develop flight control laws at 20 predetermined transonic and supersonic flight-test conditions (9 transonic and 11 supersonic) at an estimated cost of $2.4 million under a Boeing interdivisional work authorization (IWA).
2. Verify and validate Boeing module and Flight control electronic set Automated Software Test (FAST) using Matrix X autocoder at an estimated cost of $1.67 million.

Results

1. Boeing developed AAW control laws at 18 flight-test conditions (2 supersonic flight-test conditions were eliminated because they could not be achieved in level flight) using NASTRAN, ISMD, Matrix X, MODSDF, and MATLAB. Actual costs totaled $2.2 million under the Boeing IWA. NASA used CONDUIT to develop a set of control laws to maximize performance and limit loads.
2. Boeing module and FAST verification and validation testing actually cost $1.9 million.

Lessons Learned

Different sets of control laws using slightly different control usage sets obtained satisfactory roll performance at most flight conditions. Initial AAW F-18 flight research testing produced higher-than-predicted roll rates. AAW technology was successfully proven in full scale, but the effort experienced some cost increases.

Item 2-8
Flight research instrumentation.

Goals
The AAW team planned to install instrumentation comparable to that used in previous F-18 loads flight-test aircraft. The project allocated $170,000 for instrumentation in the original budget.

Results
NASA provided an additional $200,000 for instrumentation. This resulted in a full suite of instrumentation including a flight data management system, accelerometers, strain gages, and control surface position sensors.

Lessons Learned
1. Planners did not adequately consider instrumentation requirements early in program.
2. Planners should have programmed a work breakdown structure task to determine correct types and quantity of instrumentation needed.
3. The project benefited greatly from having a partner (NASA) willing to cover this expense.
4. Ultimately, the aircraft was sufficiently instrumented to meet program requirements.

Item 2-9
AAW design process (aero/loads database development).

Goals
Start with existing databases, then analytically modify and augment them.

Results
Parameter identification (PID) flight testing was used primarily to reduce structural loads risk beyond what was reasonably achievable through analysis.

Lessons Learned
1. Timely design confidence is more effectively obtained through PID early in the flight-test program.
2. Key technical contributors (i.e., good loads and aero databases) need to be well understood in order to conduct a useful experiment.

3: Ground Testing

Item 3-1
Premodification wing-stiffness testing.

Goals
Conduct a wing-stiffness test early in the program in order to characterize wing bending and torsional stiffness of the preproduction F-18 wing with Roll I and Roll II modifications, prior to AAW modifications.

Results
Researchers completed premodification stiffness tests and characterized baseline stiffness of a preproduction F-18 wing that had experienced a significant number of flight hours. This proved very important because baseline upper aft box wing cover fastener holes had elongated following years of flight and maintenance.

Lessons Learned
1. Never assume analyses unsupported by tests will be accurate. Wing-stiffness tests may be time consuming but proved valuable to the AAW program.
2. Other aircraft research programs would undoubtedly benefit from similar wing tests.

Item 3-2
Postmodification wing-stiffness testing.

Goals
Boeing planned to conduct a wing-stiffness test to characterize wing bending and torsional stiffness of the F-18 wing following AAW modifications.

Results
NASA and Boeing completed postmodification wing-stiffness tests and characterized AAW F-18 wing stiffness. Pretest analysis had predicted a 17-percent reduction in stiffness, but comparison of pre- and postmodification tests showed an approximately 12-percent difference in torsional stiffness due to fastener hole elongation. NASA also accomplished extensive load calibration testing.

Lessons Learned
1. The AAW wing modification resulted in a 5-percent effective reduction in wing stiffness.
2. This test proved that the AAW modification had returned the test bed wing to the required stiffness level (as found on the preproduction F-18), and that the AAW wing met program requirements with regard to buckling and flutter characteristics.

Item 3-3
Modal survey.

Goals
Boeing planned to conduct a vibration test to characterize the test bed aircraft's natural frequencies and modes.

Results
A vibration test performed by NASA Dryden determined natural frequencies/ modes of F-18 AAW test bed.

Lessons Learned
1. F-18 AAW modal characteristics varied only slightly from those of the standard F-18.
2. This test established a degree of confidence in flutter/aeroservoelastic (ASE) analysis and flight-test clearance.

Item 3-4

Structural mode interaction (SMI) tests and flutter/ASE Phase 1 flight maneuvers.

Goals

Boeing was to conduct an SMI test to gather no-wind response data to anchor aeroservoelastic predictive analyses.

Results

NASA Dryden performed the SMI test.

Lessons Learned

1. SMI results compared reasonably well with predictions. Differences between predictive models and ground-test results were important measures to use for flight data analysis.
2. OBES excitation was critical for derivation of in-flight transfer functions as comparisons to predictions (ASE model validation).
3. Levels of uncertainty derived from ASE model-SMI and model-flight differences were important indicators of data quality. Relatively poor-quality data was gathered at low-altitude subsonic turbulence conditions, which biased the transfer functions to produce conservative results for Phase 2 guidance.
4. Phase 2 flight control laws were impacted by Phase 1 ASE flight data.
5. The Phase 2 test plan was impacted by Phase 1 ASE results with regard to providing subsonic ASE clearance for Phase 2 flight tests.

4: Flight Testing

Item 4-1

Decision to fly the AAW experiment rather than explore the technology through ground experiments alone.

Goals

AAW technical development was already matured via both analysis and elaborate wind tunnel testing. Flight-test anchored adjustment factors were already available for conventional controls. Key characteristics, especially Reynolds number, were not well represented in scale models. Elevated loads were not available with scaled aeroelastic wind tunnel models. Full-scale flight-testing offered the best opportunity for validating AAW technology for future applications.

Results

Advocates of the AAW project argued convincingly that a full-scale, piloted demonstrator would produce the most useful flight-test results. Internal politics and competition for funding necessitated tailoring the proposal for any given audience, but project advocates always kept in mind the technical reasons that formed the basis for the continual press toward flight testing.

Lessons Learned

Always have a solid understanding of the engineering reasons why flight testing is necessary so that when arguments arise, the project is solidly justified from a technical standpoint. Allow senior management to tailor the proposal to best reach the audience that they are lobbying for support. Coordinate with the organization that will conduct the flight testing in order to assure that all the correct arguments, interagency support, and shared resources are committed before open competition for funding goes public.

Item 4-2
Aerodynamic data and modeling.

Goals
Boeing planned to use the established aerodynamic database and modify it with analytical results. Boeing planned to use A4 loads flight-test data to improve the analytical loads model.

Results
Boeing updated the data based on Phase I PID flights, but the A4 data was insufficient, so the company used results from the PID flights to create loads models.

Lessons Learned
Based on pilot comments, it seems clear that the aerodynamic model for the AAW aircraft should have better fidelity information for each control effector. Traditional models with performance based on multiple control-effector inputs do a poor job of predicting the effect of individual control surfaces.

Item 4-3
AAW flight simulation.

Goals
The research team planned to use a multistep approach to modify the existing aerodynamics database with flex increments generated by aeroelastic analysis and update it with data from the PID test flights.

Results
A flight-simulation program was developed using the modified database.

Lessons Learned
The research pilots found that the simulation provided an accurate prediction of actual aircraft performance and flying qualities.

Item 4-4
Test bed flying qualities.

Goals
Provide acceptable flying qualities, but not at the expense of fully investigating the implementation of AAW technology.

Results
AAW control laws exhibited Level I (clearly adequate for the mission flight phase) flying qualities during simulation and flight, except for some transonic test points where roll rates, though improved, were less than desired for an operational aircraft (but not less than expected).

Lessons Learned
Based on pilot comments, the AAW flight control laws provided acceptable flying qualities. The aircraft's response was smooth and predictable. No delays or ratcheting were evident, and predictability allowed for precise bank captures.

Item 4-5
Roll performance.

Goals
Develop AAW technology to provide acceptable roll rates at all transonic and supersonic flight conditions within the limits of the modified F-18 test bed. Disable the rolling tail function provided by the differential stabilator.

Results
Overall transonic roll rates using AAW control laws were considerably higher than those achieved with the original F-18 aircraft control laws. Some transonic roll rates were less than required, but this could be improved with a full application of AAW technology in a new airframe.

Lessons Learned
Although aircraft roll performance was generally acceptable, some roll rates were unacceptably slow for aggressive maneuvering. Because the simulations predicted these performance points, research pilots were able to adjust their flight profiles accordingly.

Item 4-6
Test bed limitations.

Goals
Use an existing supersonic aircraft as a test bed for AAW flight research.

Results
The F-18 proved to be the best available candidate, though it was often operating at the edge of its performance envelope. This greatly reduced the efficiency of the test flights.

Lessons Learned
1. Future tests should be accomplished using an aircraft that does not need to fly at the limits of its capabilities.
2. Unanticipated pitot static accuracy problems in the supersonic regime caused researchers to adopt a GPS work-around solution to determining altitude. This would be less of a problem with a full-envelope flight control system.

5: Flight-Test Results

Item 5-1
Parameter identification test flights using the F-18 Systems Research Aircraft (SRA).

Goals
This option was not in the original research plan.

Results
Added to program in CY 2000, this approach provided a huge risk-reduction factor for later AAW flights. SRA flight data added confidence to proceed during the first flight readiness review.

Lessons Learned
Never miss an opportunity to reduce risk by testing a technical idea on a tried-and-true flight test bed. It could save costs later.

Item 5-2
Aileron effectiveness.

Goals
Incorporate aileron effectiveness in the AAW control laws.

Results
Programmers designed the control laws to use both aileron and trailing-edge inboard (TEI) flaps to control loads at high speeds during supersonic flight.

Lessons Learned
At one supersonic test point, collective gain for the trailing edges increased sideslip excursion.

Item 5-3
TEI flap control surfaces.

Goals
Develop control laws for using the TEI flaps for AAW load control.

Results
Used both ailerons and TEI flaps to control loads supersonically at high dynamic pressures.

Lessons Learned
With Boeing AAW control laws, the TEI flaps were not as effective supersonically for lateral control. At Test Point 17, the collective gain for trailing edges increased sideslip, either because of vehicle asymmetry or due to flow from the trailing-edge flap affecting the vertical tail.

Item 5-4
LEI flap control surfaces.

Goals
In the AAW configuration, the LEI flaps would be used similarly to those in the baseline F-18.

Results
The LEI control surfaces were modified with increased travel in AAW gearing function optimization. This was achievable at minimal cost because the original design allowed increased travel.

Lessons Learned
When used up to 5 degrees, the LEI flaps contributed to roll rates. This modification would probably not have been pursued if hardware modifications were required.

Item 5-5
LEO control surfaces.

Goals
Develop AAW control laws for effective use of LEO flaps.

Results
AAW control laws effectively exploited the LEO flaps.

Lessons Learned
At certain speeds, the effectiveness of both the LEO flaps and ailerons are about equal.

Item 5-6
Test vehicle asymmetry.

Lessons Learned
1. When used with ISMD, NASA lateral-directional three-degrees-of-freedom linear-design aerodynamics did not sufficiently represent the test vehicle's lateral-directional asymmetry with regards to roll rate as modeled in NASA's PID-derived nonlinear aerodynamics. The baseline production F-18 does not have this magnitude of asymmetry.
2. Several Boeing point-design control laws produced excessive sideslip for left full-stick rolls.
3. NASA designed its control laws with nonlinear aero for a roll rate sign having the worst bare airframe flying qualities. If asymmetry was inherent to a design, solutions for the use of linear design aero could also be formulated. There is nothing about AAW that inherently introduces the asymmetry that was encountered in flight testing.
4. Not all researchers agreed that asymmetry was to blame. Robert Clarke and Ryan Dibley, with associated researchers, pointed out that early F-18 wind tunnel tests showed that the trailing-edge flaps deflected airflow into the vertical tails that created yawing moments greater than the capability of the rudder to counteract. For the X-53, the Boeing aerodynamic model predicted almost no sideslip, while the Dryden model predicted 2.8 degrees of sideslip (proverse yaw). Flight data indicated a worse-than-predicted proverse yaw tendency, apparently confirming the wind tunnel results.

Item 5-7

Linear loads model.

Lessons Learned

ISMD hinge-moment constraints should be included for each optimized control surface effector. Test vehicle asymmetry revealed the need for inclusion of a rudder hinge-moment constraint in ISMD, which had not been included in the linear design loads model.

Item 5-8
AAW control law architecture compatibility with ISMD optimization.

Lessons Learned
AAW control architecture should be modified for improved compatibility with the current ISMD optimization. There are two areas for architectural compatibility improvement:

1. Include the input source signal to the ISMD normal acceleration (Nz) proportional gains (PKx).
2. Include saturation limiting of the immediate outputs of ISMD roll rate feedback gains RKx.

Item 5-9
Design aerodynamics approximating actual aerodynamics.

Lessons Learned
The positive feedback control law architecture and the current ISMD method, which suggested this implementation, are very dependent on accurate design aerodynamics (especially effector surface control power).

6: Program Management

Item 6-1
Solicitation instrument: Program Research Development Announcement (PRDA).

Goals
The AAW research plan called for substantial, complex modification of a supersonic fighter jet. Use of a PRDA offered contractors increased flexibility in proposing their technical approaches. The effort was based on a competitive-bid, cost-plus-fixed-fee (CPFF) work breakdown structure (WBS). Cost estimates were to be submitted within 60 days.

Results
The WBS was thorough, and it covered all aircraft modification tasks. The plan only had to be modified slightly over the 5-year contract period. The WBS had to be rebaselined twice to account for optimistic cost estimates, increased Government requirements, and other unforeseen technical problems encountered on subcontracts for flight computer and actuator modification.

Lessons Learned
1. The CPFF contract/competitive-bid approach resulted in a low estimate of project costs. These costs should not have been used as an initial program baseline. The Government's baseline should reflect reasonable cost levels, which are often difficult to determine depending on the risks and uncertainties associated with the project.
2. The Government funding organization must be ready to live up to the CPFF nature of the work, and budget accordingly.

Item 6-2
Cost-plus-fixed-fee contract.

Goals
Under a CPFF contract, the contractor is paid a negotiated amount regardless of incurred expenses. The low bid reflected the $11.8 million in available funds listed in the PRDA.

Results
All of the WBS items for major modification tasks associated with AAW were subject to cost increases. Total Air Force costs for the program grew to $13.86 million. Ground-test support had to shift to NASA within the Government partnership agreement.

Lessons Learned
1. Cost growth is inevitable under a CPFF approach. A fixed-price approach would force contractors to sharpen their cost estimates.
2. The timeline for preparing cost proposals would need to be extended. A fixed-price effort would have likely cost around $17 million, but it may have included ground-test costs.

Item 6-3

Overall program costs.

Goals

Estimated Air Force costs totaled approximately $12 million, and estimated NASA costs totaled approximately $12 million. Total estimated joint cost was $24 million.

Results

1. Air Force costs included a $13.86 million contract to Boeing and a $1.57 million Military Interdepartmental Purchase Request (MIPR) to NASA.
2. NASA direct costs (1997–2004) totaled $12.23 million plus $1.45 million for NASA range support.

Lessons Learned

1. Research of this type usually results in cost growth and must be anticipated in out-year budgets.
2. Cost totals for AAW research were less than 50 percent of contract costs for previous technology demonstration programs such as the X-29 Forward Swept Wing and X-45 Unmanned Combat Air Vehicle.
3. Costs increase as the program schedule is spread over multiple years due to annual funding limits.

Item 6-4

Government-supplier relationships.

Goals

Planners examined several options for project management:
1. The integrated product-development team (IPT)
2. The customer/prime contractor/subcontractors
3. The consortium, with Government agency as integrator

Ultimately, they selected an IPT approach featuring an Air Force–NASA partnership via a Memorandum of Understanding. In the jointly funded program, NASA operations were funded through NASA plus Air Force MIPR. The Air Force contracted Boeing to modify the test bed and manage subcontractors. NASA also established a support contract with Boeing.

Results

Cost, schedule, and performance were reasonably well integrated, but the program could have used an overarching master schedule. NASA drove the overall project schedule, which was not entirely in line with the Boeing–Air Force contract schedule. The NASA schedule included additional tasks beyond those included in Boeing's contract with the Air Force. NASA paid the cost of these added requirements and picked up the additional workload when cost increases prevented delivery of the original Air Force contract. Boeing performed analyses and aircraft modifications, and it helped conduct tests.

Lessons Learned
1. The AAW IPT had a number of technical advantages and disadvantages, but it generally excelled.
2. Mutual trust and schedule flexibility between Air Force, NASA, and Boeing program managers were crucial to success.
3. The funding pace gave the program time to work out issues.
4. A master schedule integrated across all stakeholders would have helped, along with a simpler, more timely mechanism for making contract changes.

Item 6-5
Class II modification requirements.

Goals
Class II modifications in the Contract Data Requirements List (CDRL), a list of the data deliverables to be produced by the contractor, required inclusion of preliminary and final design data, performance, stability and control, mass properties, power, safety analyses, airworthiness, and operating limits.

Results
Boeing increased safety planning to incorporate operational risk-management techniques. All analyses and tests were conducted, documented, and delivered by the supplier in the contractor's format.

Lessons Learned
The Class II modification process produced an essential set of reports containing all analyses and test data needed to support mission success and flight-safety decisions.

Item 6-6
Cost reporting.

Goals
Contract CDRL required use of Earned Value Management principles via cost schedule status reporting (CSSR). This is required by law on all contracts that exceed a prescribed dollar threshold.

Results
Program managers used CSSR tied to WBS aircraft-modification tasks. CSSR is somewhat useful on research and development efforts, but delays of a month or more render it inadequate as a useful, action-oriented tool. Use of CSSR forced several rebaseline efforts that cost the program time and money.

Lessons Learned
1. The CSSR approach should be modified to accommodate some relaxation of the rules to allow timely adjustment to WBS work packages.
2. The CSSR system is difficult for contractors to use in research efforts. Contractor internal rules imposed unwieldy review processes on AAW program managers. Contractor program managers could not implement changes quickly enough to keep CSSR reporting relevant.
3. There is currently no way to exempt contractors from this requirement, but the limits of CSSR should be recognized.
4. Assessment of obsolete CSSR data by a financial analyst without knowledge of overall program progress and technical metrics are useless and should be disregarded.

Item 6-7
Expenditure reporting.

Goals
The CDRL required contractor submission of monthly contract vouchers.

Results
Expenditure metrics were tracked using monthly reports. These vouchers were necessary because Defense Finance and Accounting Service (DFAS) reporting lagged by 2 or more months.

Lessons Learned
Do not depend on DFAS expenditure information because it significantly lags behind current conditions. The DFAS often pays bills from funding supplied during several previous fiscal years. DFAS reports are, at times, inaccurate and unreliable.

Item 6-8
Funding profiles.

Goals
A majority of Air Force funding was attained via Program Element (PE) 63211F, augmented with funds from two other 6.3 PEs. NASA funding and in-house efforts helped sustain final modifications, ground testing, and flight-test operations.

Results
Sufficient funds were obtained to complete the basic flight research program. As is often the case with Government efforts, funding profiles available to accomplish the budgeted cost of work scheduled were less than optimal.

Lessons Learned
Optimal funding profiles would result in improved program cost efficiencies. The Program Objective Memorandum (POM) and Budget Estimate Submission (BES) process, coupled with decisions to balance funding across active programs, rarely provides optimal funding profiles, and it results in increased overall costs to Government programs.

7: Integrated Product Team

Item 7-1
Integrated product-development team charter.

Goals
A charter clarified program goals, exit strategy, and resources required from the funding organizations. Further, it committed the organization, to the extent possible, to meeting the program resource needs. The AAW program manager developed the IPT charter to define the following:
- Team name
- Date of charter
- Team members
- Mission statement
- Organizational fit
- Performance goals
- End product
- Background
- Team ground rules

Results
The Air Force IPT charter described support needed from the various technical divisions at AFRL. During the flight-test program, there were only two or three AFRL technical personnel supporting the project. During the AFW wind tunnel studies, there was support from the aerodynamics, flight controls, and structures and dynamics divisions. During the flight-test program, however, the flight controls group never implemented the IPT charter.

Lessons Learned
Failure to understand the charter's value resulted in organizational failure to adopt prescribed standards that would have been beneficial to the program.

Item 7-2
Formation and development of a multi-agency team.

Goals
No single aeroelastic research group in any one Government agency had the resources to mount a flight-test program for AAW. AFRL, Langley, and Rockwell had to join their resources to make the initial aeroelastic wind tunnel program possible. The ultimate goal eventually became development of a Government/industry team capable of executing an AAW flight program to prove the technology in full scale.

Results
Grassroots efforts by aeroelasticians in industry, NASA, and the Air Force developed a working level interest in AAW technology among these organizations. Study contracts generated non-inventor interest for industry support, and the results provided an outline for the flight-test program that convinced AFRL leadership that it should be a sponsor. Despite evidence of some friction resulting from past AFRL-NASA joint efforts, Air Force and industry advocates convinced NASA to join the partnership. Researchers from Dryden were the first onboard. Those at NASA Langley appeared somewhat reluctant to support Dryden, until parallel aeroelastic control derivative model programs gave them a reason to join. Contractor consolidation complicated creating the contractor portion of the team. Through mergers, the McDonnell Douglas–Rockwell team eventually became part of Boeing. An abundance of good technical reasons for pursuing the flight-test option gave AAW unstoppable momentum.

Lessons Learned
1. Technical interest, perceived value to the industry, and timing were essential elements in attaining the cooperation of all stakeholders. It was important to get the technical questions answered, network among multiple agencies, and develop interest and support as early as possible.
2. Informally work out any problems or obstacles to establishing a joint effort early and behind the scenes.
3. Use Phase 6.2 study (feasibility study and option down-select) money to develop contractor interest, and get as many contractors as the budget will stand.
4. As long as the basic technical questions get answered, let each part of a multi-agency/contractor team work their own technical agenda. This gives the agencies/contractors additional incentive to support the project.

5. Senior leadership should work to breach stovepipes and foster cooperation. Inspire continued support by briefing all interested parties on progress, results, and benefits of the program. Spread kudos to all who deserve them.

6. Ensure that the program has a definite end in sight so that all team members anticipate a positive payout. This assures senior leadership that they are not mortgaging their future budgets.

7. Years of advance preparation, including contractor development, analytical studies, wind tunnel tests, etc., and the relationships developed during these preliminary research efforts helped forge a successful team.

8. Air Force leadership, supported heavily by the contractor, was crucial to solidifying the team. Selection of a NASA-owned F-18 as the test bed was a key ingredient in retaining NASA support.

9. Timing was also essential. During other years, higher priority programs are likely to have displaced this innovative "tech push" effort. This novel program succeeded, in part, because it was small enough to avoid excessive scrutiny that may have resulted in budget cuts.

Recommendations and Conclusions

Taking into account the results of the AAW flight research program, the project team recommended in their final report that the use of AAW technology be considered for application to any new flight vehicle design where significant aeroelastic effects are expected. More important, they noted, "AAW technology should be considered an enabler for expanding the feasible aircraft design space in terms of wing thickness-to-chord and aspect ratios and tailless configurations to achieve overall performance."[18]

Researchers identified two key issues that suggested design process improvements that would facilitate the use of AAW technology on future aircraft. First, designers need to embrace structural flexibility effects and exploit their potential benefits. Aircraft characteristics that would be imparted to an aircraft designed with AAW technology in mind include lighter structural weight and improved maneuver performance, as well as reduced drag, and structural loads. But the adoption of structural flexibility as the primary control effector poses challenges to the current design philosophy in which wind tunnel data serves as the basis for aerodynamic and loads database development. Linear aeroelastic analysis may not be sufficient to correct for minor flexibility effects. To address this issue, the AAW research team recommended a three-step process.[19]

1. Perform pressure model wind tunnel testing and apply improved linear aerodynamic correction tools using wind tunnel pressure data to improve the aeroelastic analysis predictions used for developing control law design and loads analysis models.
2. Apply improved aeroelastic computational fluid dynamics (CFD) tools with detailed structural dynamic finite element models to develop nonlinear aeroelastic databases supporting flight simulation.
3. Perform parameter identification flight testing to refine aerodynamic and loads databases for simulation.[20]

The second issue was concerned with control law design. Researchers noted that the Boeing design process as implemented did not initially produce a control law. Instead, control designers were given a set of potentially nonlinear control surface gearing functions and left to consider how best to implement these in an actual control law. Gearing function design did not directly address control law requirements, and so evaluation of simulation models resulted in

---

18. Field et al., "The Active Aeroelastic Wing (AAW) Flight Research Program, the X-53—Final Report," p. 325–326.
19. Ibid., p. 326.
20. Ibid.

various trim optimization compromises. The NASA Dryden team was able to directly produce a control law because the CONDUIT tool performed a constrained optimization of the control system. As described in the team's final report, "Tighter integration of control law design within the AAW design process would produce better first time quality."[21]

In conclusion, the AAW flight research program successfully demonstrated the technology in full scale, proving that it is possible to exploit aeroelastic effects for a net benefit. Research results generated a flight-test database for correlation with wind tunnel data and analytical predictions. According to Pete Flick, "the correlation of those data sets will be developed into design guidelines for future applications of the technology."[22]

Ed Pendleton led a team made up of Air Force, NASA, and industry to develop and promote the AAW concept for more than two decades, and he is quick to point out its historic roots. "The Wright brothers were the first to use wing flexibility and wing twist in their wing-warping concept," he explained. "It was novel in 1903 and it has essentially taken us 100 years to come back to it and try to use wing flexibility for the benefit of aircraft design.... We're hoping this program will break the current paradigms for wing design and essentially change the way wing designs are viewed in the future."[23]

21. Ibid.

22. Levine, "Phase Two: Effectiveness of wing twist for roll control will be explored," p. 4.

23. Christian Gelzer and Jay Levine, "Re-Wright: Wing design of the future borrows from original flyer," *X-Press*, Special Active Aeroelastic Wing Edition, NASA Dryden Flight Research Center (December 17, 2003): p. 5.

APPENDIX 1:
Flight-Test Log

NASA Dryden received F-18A (Navy Bu. No. 161744) on March 4, 1999, and gave it NASA tail number 853. It was later modified for the AAW flight research program, which was divided into two phases. Phase 1 (Block 1) included functional check flights, aircraft maneuvering, flutter/aeroservoelastic (ASE) envelope clearance, and simulated outboard leading-edge flap (OLEF) failures. Phase 1 (Block 2) consisted of air data calibration flights to ensure accurate measurement of aircraft velocity, Mach number, angle of attack, and sideslip during flight tests. Phase 1 (Block 3) parameter identification flights were used to update the existing aerodynamic database, eliminate database deficiencies, and improve the loads database for development of AAW control laws. A total of 50 Phase 1 flights plus one follow-on sortie were accomplished between November 15, 2002, and June 25, 2003. Phase 2 consisted of 34 AAW control law development flights plus one follow-on sortie that were accomplished between December 14, 2004, and April 11, 2005. Dana Purifoy and Dick Ewers served as project pilots. The highly modified test aircraft, with its unique research flight control system, was redesignated X-53 on August 16, 2006, per memo by the Air Force Deputy Chief of Staff, Strategic Plans and Programs.[1] It was subsequently named the Full-scale Advanced Systems Testbed (FAST), and used for control system development in the Integrated Resilient Aircraft Control (IRAC) project, sponsored by NASA's Aviation Safety Program.[2] This flight log encompasses all sorties undertaken during the span of the AAW flight research program.

---

1. Holly Jordan, "Active Aeroelastic Wing flight research vehicle receives X-53 designation," *http://www.wpafb.af.mil/news/story.asp?id=123035661*, December 11, 2006, accessed May 20, 2012.
2. Curt Hansen, Jacob Schaefer, John J. Burken, Marcus Johnson, and Nhan Nguyen, "Handling Qualities Evaluations of Low Complexity Model Reference Adaptive Controllers for Reduced Pitch and Roll Damping Scenarios," AIAA Guidance, Navigation, and Control Conference, August 2011.

#, Date, Pilot	Objectives	Comments
AAW Phase 1 (Block 1)		
Flight #1 15 NOV 02 Purifoy	Perform functional check flight (FCF), flutter clearance for two baseline test points, and OLEF failure emulation maneuvers in auto flaps-up (AFU) for –3, –6, and –10 degree deflections.	Loss of GPS/Inertial Navigation System (INS) data and telemetry link (TM2) during engine startup. Restored prior to takeoff. Pilot noted no adverse handling qualities. Minor asymmetric buffet on left wing. Maximum altitude was 25,997 feet. Maximum speed was 361 knots (Mach 0.86). A maximum normal load factor of 3 g's was achieved. A maximum angle of attack (AOA) of 20.5 degrees was obtained. Flight time: 1.14 hours.
Flight #2 19 NOV 02 Ewers	ASE/flutter envelope expansion, and to checkout aircraft operation in standard flight controls (701E) compared to research flight control system (RFCS).	Afterburner takeoff. Pilot noted left wing higher than right at high throttle settings. Completed the ASE/flutter test points for the first two subsonic AAW test points, began flight controls investigation, and performed part of an integrated FCF maneuver. The flight was cut short due to a chase aircraft Fuel Low caution. Maximum altitude was 16,600 feet. Maximum speed was 485 knots (Mach 0.91). A maximum normal load factor of 5 g's was achieved. A maximum AOA of 10 degrees was obtained. Flight time: 0.98 hours.
Flight #3 19 NOV 02 Purifoy	Continue with ASE/flutter envelope expansion checkout aircraft operation in standard flight controls (701E) compared to RFCS. For this flight, the takeoff envelope airspeed limit was 445 knots indicated airspeed (KIAS).	Completed ASE/flutter test points for three subsonic AAW test points and further investigated aircraft operation in standard flight controls (701E) compared to RFCS. Reversion check could not be accomplished due to missed onboard excitation system (OBES) engagement step. During the attempted maneuver, aileron hinge-moment load was approximately 100 percent of the Flight Operating Limit. Maximum altitude and velocity were 15,240 feet and 533 knots (Mach 0.96). A maximum normal load factor of 5 g's was achieved. A maximum AOA of 8.6 degrees was obtained. Flight time: 0.88 hours.

#, Date, Pilot	Objectives	Comments
Flight #4 26 NOV 02 Ewers	Continue flutter envelope expansion with integrated FCF maneuvers.	Continued expanding the envelope for ASE/flutter and performed an integrated FCF maneuver. During this flight, maximum altitude and velocity were 12,340 feet and 594 knots (Mach 0.97). A maximum normal load factor of 2.5 g's was achieved. A maximum AOA of 8.2 degrees was obtained. Flight time: 0.81 hours.
Flight #5 26 NOV 02 Purifoy	Finish ASE/flutter envelope expansion with repeats, and perform integrated FCF maneuvers, OLEF failure emulation maneuver with half flaps, a tower fly-by, and a couple of 5-g windup turns (WUTs) for symmetric loads investigation.	Completed ASE/flutter envelope expansion test points with repeats and integrated FCF maneuver. Pilot noted slight roll-off during OLEF failure emulation maneuvers. Performed two tower fly-bys to Mach 0.8 and 0.9 and two 5-g WUTs for symmetric loads investigation. Maximum altitude and velocity were 25,330 feet and 595 knots (Mach 0.98). A maximum normal load factor of 5.2 g's was achieved. A maximum AOA of 10.2 degrees was obtained. Flight time: 0.97 hours.
AAW Phase 1 (Block 2)		
Flight #6 10 DEC 02 Ewers	Perform air data calibration maneuvers.	Pilot reported that during acceleration to 0.97 Mach, the altimeter wound off about 300 feet. During repositioning turns throughout the flight, the pilot hovered around the 45-degree angle of bank (AOB) limit, sometimes reaching up to 48 degrees AOB. During this flight, maximum altitude and velocity were 16,205 feet and 598 knots (Mach 0.98). A maximum normal load factor of 4.6 g's was achieved. A maximum AOA of 12.3 degrees was obtained. Flight time: 1.0 hour.

#, Date, Pilot	Objectives	Comments
Flight #7 10 DEC 02 Purifoy	Perform final air data calibration maneuvers.	Completed air data calibration maneuvers with repeats. Pilot reported both Mach and altimeter jump during high beta (sideslip). During this flight, maximum altitude and velocity were 16,240 feet and 592 knots (Mach 0.97). A maximum normal load factor of 4.4 g's was achieved. A maximum AOA of 7.5 degrees was obtained. Flight time: 1.0 hour.
AAW Phase 1 (Block 3)		
Flight #8 20 DEC 02 Ewers	Repeat OLEF failure emulation in AFU, perform OLEF failure emulation at full flaps, and begin parameter identification (PID) for AAW subsonic test conditions.	Pilot noted that he could see the deflections but felt nothing in the cockpit. Roll power was smooth at 7.4 to 7.5 degrees AOA. Slight buffet at 8.0 to 8.2 degrees AOA. Aircraft was responsive and easily controllable. Differential doublets seemed to have more roll at Mach 0.85 than at Mach 0.88. During this flight, maximum altitude and velocity were 26,000 feet and 503 knots (Mach 0.97). A maximum normal load factor of 5.1 g's was achieved. A maximum AOA of 11.1 degrees was obtained. Flight time: 0.9 hours.
Flight #9 20 DEC 02 Purifoy	Repeat the OLEF failure emulation with full flaps, perform a loads/handling qualities integrated test block at 15,000 feet and Mach 0.95, continue with subsonic PID maneuvers, and begin subsonic loads model verification maneuvers.	Stable, light buffeting, and a little right wing drop. Flow separation at 10 degrees AOA. Postflight comments included a suggestion that the pilots may need a few minutes between rolls and that aircraft unload from the rolls is odd, that 7/8-stick rolls are difficult and unrepeatable, and that the aileron may have been stalling during some maneuvers. During this flight, maximum altitude and velocity were 25,916 feet and 505 knots (Mach 0.98). A maximum normal load factor of 5.1 g's was achieved. A maximum AOA of 10.5 degrees was obtained. Flight time: 1.0 hour.

#, Date, Pilot	Objectives	Comments
Flight #10 24 JAN 03 Ewers	Perform an aircraft checkout Integrated Test Block (ITB) at 5,000 feet and Mach 0.95, and continue with OBES PID and loads model verification maneuvers.	After startup, the leading-edge flap (LEF) was split, producing a FLAPS OFF caution and preventing the pilot from resetting the flight controls until the pilot put the flight control system (FCS) in OVERRIDE. During aileron maneuver with ½-lateral-stick, 360-degree roll, the RFCS disengaged. The full-stick 4-g rolling pullout maneuver exceeded 110 percent of the hinge-moment load limit, and the control room called return to base (RTB). During this flight, maximum altitude and velocity were 18,490 feet and 597 knots (Mach 0.98). A maximum normal load factor of 5.2 g's was achieved. A maximum AOA of 6.2 degrees was obtained. Flight time: 0.7 hours.
Flight #11 24 JAN 03 Ewers	Continue with OBES PID maneuvers at 15,000 feet and Mach 0.95, and begin the final aircraft checkout ITB at 5,000 feet and 0.85 Mach.	During execution of the aircraft Day-of-Flight and Pilot Checklist procedures, the control room observed an anomaly with the FCS display. One maneuver produced a high aileron hinge moment (approximately 108 percent). During an ITB reversion check, right wing fold bending/torque exceeded 110 percent and the control room called RTB. During this flight, maximum flight conditions were not recorded. Flight time: 0.4 hours.
Flight #12 07 FEB 03 Purifoy	Continue with OBES PID maneuvers and perform repeats of loads model verification maneuvers to investigate NzW (the product of normal acceleration [Nz] and gross weight [W]) effects in AAW component loads.	The pilot performed an OBES maneuver to verify that the left digital display indicator (DDI) was adequate for flight without the right DDI warnings/advisories interfering with any visual cues on the left DDI. During this flight, maximum altitude and velocity were 15,480 feet and 542 knots (Mach 0.96). A maximum normal load factor of 5.2 g's was achieved. A maximum AOA of 9.4 degrees was obtained. Flight time: 0.9 hours.

#, Date, Pilot	Objectives	Comments
Flight #13 18 FEB 03 Purifoy	Continue OBES PID maneuvers.	Completed OBES PID maneuvering at three flight conditions. Embedded GPS/INS (EGI) was not functional. During this flight, maximum altitude and velocity were 10,382 feet and 588 knots (0.96 Mach). A maximum normal load factor of 4 g's was achieved. A maximum AOA of 7.4 degrees was obtained. Flight time: 0.7 hours.
Flight #14 19 FEB 03 Purifoy	Complete OBES PID maneuvers and continue with loads model verification buildup maneuvers.	Completed OBES PID for the AAW subsonic envelope and performed repeats of rolls with incremental stick inputs. During this flight, maximum altitude and velocity were 11,639 feet and 597 knots (Mach 0.98). A maximum normal load factor of 5 g's was achieved. A maximum AOA of 7.2 degrees was obtained. Flight time: 0.6 hours.
Flight #15 20 FEB 03 Purifoy	Continue with loads model verification maneuvers within the AAW subsonic envelope.	Performed 360-degree rolls, 5-g windup turns, and 4-g rolling pullouts. Repeated OBES PID collective maneuvers at 5,000 feet and Mach 0.85, and performed rolls at 10,000 feet and Mach 0.7 for comparison with Systems Research Aircraft (SRA) flight results. During this flight, maximum altitude and velocity were 11,215 feet and 562 knots (Mach 0.96). A maximum normal load factor of 4.6 g's was achieved. A maximum AOA of 8.4 degrees was obtained. Flight time: 0.8 hours.

#, Date, Pilot	Objectives	Comments
Flight #16 20 FEB 03 Ewers	Perform maneuver repeats of OBES PID, 360-degree rolls, and 4-g rolling pullouts at select AAW test conditions and some SRA test conditions.	RFCS could not be engaged during flight, impeding the execution of OBES PID repeat maneuvers. Rolls and rolling pullouts were performed at four AAW flight conditions. Some rolling maneuvers were also performed at two SRA flight conditions. During this flight, maximum altitude and velocity were 25,000 feet and 600 knots (Mach 0.98). A maximum normal load factor of 5.4 g's was achieved. A maximum AOA of 9.2 degrees was obtained. Flight time: 0.8 hours.
Flight #17 04 MAR 03 Ewers	Begin, gather PID data from OBES maneuvers at various supersonic flight conditions, perform aircraft checkout, and complete the final FCF maneuver (rolling pullout maneuvers [RPM] lockup test).	Research maneuvering was restricted to straight and level flight. The pilot commented that the airplane performed well supersonically, with no trim issues. During this flight, maximum altitude and velocity were 35,936 feet and 558 knots (Mach 1.28). A maximum normal load factor of 2.6 g's was achieved. A maximum AOA of 6.5 degrees was obtained. Flight time: 0.5 hours.
Flight #18 06 March 03 Purifoy	Continue with supersonic flutter/ASE and loads clearance, and perform aircraft RFCS checkout.	Rolls were performed with incremental stick inputs. RTB initiated due to chase aircraft in-flight emergency. During this flight, maximum altitude and velocity were 34,508 feet and 512 knots (Mach 1.16). A maximum normal load factor of 2.4 g's was achieved. A maximum AOA of 8.9 degrees was obtained. Flight time: 0.5 hours.
Flight #19 06 MAR 03 Purifoy	Continue with supersonic flutter/ASE and loads clearance.	Performed flutter/ASE and loads clearance maneuvers, and accomplished some AAW/SRA rolls. During this flight, maximum altitude and velocity were 40,303 feet and 555 knots (Mach 1.23). A maximum normal load factor of 5.2 g's was achieved. A maximum AOA of 8.8 degrees was obtained. Flight time: 0.7 hours.

#, Date, Pilot	Objectives	Comments
Flight #20 06 MAR 03 Ewers	Continue with supersonic flutter/ASE and loads clearance.	Performed flutter/ASE and loads clearance maneuvers, and accomplished a repeat small collective OBES PID maneuver at 10,000 feet and Mach 0.85. During this flight, maximum altitude and velocity were 28,797 feet and 567 knots (Mach 1.22). A maximum normal load factor of 4.2 g's was achieved. A maximum AOA of 11.8 degrees was obtained. Flight time: 0.5 hours.
Flight #21 11 MAR 03 Ewers	Continue with supersonic flutter/ASE and loads clearance.	Completed flutter/ASE clearance at 20,000 feet, and continued loads clearance. During this flight, maximum altitude and velocity were 25,668 feet and 565 knots (Mach 1.14). A maximum normal load factor of 5.2 g's was achieved. A maximum AOA of 7.15 degrees was obtained. Flight time: 0.4 hours.
Flight #22 11 MAR 03 Ewers	Continue with supersonic flutter/ASE and loads clearance.	During this flight, maximum altitude and velocity were 35,920 feet and 601 knots (Mach 1.33). A maximum normal load factor of 4.6 g's was achieved. A maximum AOA of 7.48 degrees was obtained. Flight time: 0.5 hours.
Flight #23 13 MAR 03 Purifoy	Continue with supersonic flutter/ASE, loads, and RFCS clearance.	During this flight, maximum altitude and velocity were 32,125 feet and 595 knots (Mach 1.34). A maximum normal load factor of 5.19 g's was achieved. A maximum AOA of 8.3 degrees was obtained. Flight time: 0.5 hours.
Flight #24 13 MAR 03 Purifoy	Continue with supersonic flutter/ASE and loads clearance.	Radio communications difficulties. During this flight, maximum altitude and velocity were 32,049 feet and 593 knots (Mach 1.32). A maximum normal load factor of 4.07 g's was achieved. A maximum AOA of 7.98 degrees was obtained. Flight time: 0.5 hours.

#, Date, Pilot	Objectives	Comments
Flight #25 13 MAR 03 Purifoy	Continue with supersonic flutter/ASE and loads clearance.	During this flight, maximum altitude and velocity were 21,305 feet and 601 knots (Mach 1.23). A maximum normal load factor of 5.29 g's was achieved. A maximum AOA of 8.56 degrees was obtained. Flight time: 0.5 hours.
Flight #26 18 MAR 03 Purifoy	Continue with supersonic flutter/ASE and loads clearance.	During this flight, maximum altitude and velocity were 19,272 feet and 612 knots (Mach 1.15). A maximum normal load factor of 5 g's was achieved. A maximum AOA of 7.7 degrees was obtained. Flight time: 0.5 hours.
Flight #27 18 MAR 03 Purifoy	Continue with supersonic flutter/ASE and loads clearance.	During this flight, maximum altitude and velocity were 24,504 feet and 648 knots (Mach 1.32). A maximum normal load factor of 5.25 g's was achieved. A maximum AOA of 7.87 degrees was obtained. Flight time: 0.5 hours.
Flight #28 19 MAR 03 Purifoy	Continue with supersonic flutter/ASE and loads clearance.	During this flight, maximum altitude and velocity were 27,138 feet and 644 knots (Mach 1.31). A maximum normal load factor of 5.1 g's was achieved. A maximum AOA of 8.2 degrees was obtained. Flight time: 0.4 hours.
Flight #29 19 MAR 03 Purifoy	Continue with supersonic flutter/ASE and loads clearance.	During this flight, maximum altitude and velocity were 27,603 feet and 632 knots (Mach 1.29). A maximum normal load factor of 5.56 g's was achieved. A maximum AOA of 8.4 degrees was obtained. Flight time: 0.4 hours.
Flight #30 20 MAR 03 Purifoy	Continue with supersonic flutter/ASE and loads clearance.	Flight cut short due to recurring built-in test logic inspect (BLIN) 321 error. During this flight, maximum altitude and velocity were 24,142 feet and 357 knots (Mach 0.83). A maximum normal load factor of 2.42 g's was achieved. A maximum AOA of 7.56 degrees was obtained. Flight time: 0.2 hours.

#, Date, Pilot	Objectives	Comments
Flight #31 25 MAR 03 Purifoy	Continue with supersonic flutter/ASE and loads clearance.	During this flight, maximum altitude and velocity were 24,863 feet and 659 knots (Mach 1.22). A maximum normal load factor of 2.88 g's was achieved. A maximum AOA of 7.78 degrees was obtained. Flight time: 0.4 hours.
Flight #32 25 MAR 03 Purifoy	Continue with supersonic flutter/ASE and loads clearance.	During this flight, maximum altitude and velocity were 22,392 feet and 651 knots (Mach 1.21). A maximum normal load factor of 4.97 g's was achieved. A maximum AOA of 8.9 degrees was obtained. Flight time: 0.5 hours.
Flight #33 25 MAR 03 Purifoy	Continue with supersonic flutter/ASE and loads clearance.	Maneuvers at 10,000 feet and Mach 1.1 and 15,000 feet and Mach 1.2 were beyond the level flight envelope for AAW. The 15,000-foot test points were performed while diving at Mach 1.2 from 18,000 feet to 13,000 feet. The 10,000-foot test points were performed at Mach 1.1 while diving from 13,000 feet to 8,000 feet. During this flight, maximum altitude and velocity were 23,489 feet and 649 knots (Mach 1.2). A maximum normal load factor of 5.19 g's was achieved. A maximum AOA of 8.87 degrees was obtained. Flight time: 0.4 hours.
Flight #34 25 MAR 03 Purifoy	Continue with supersonic flutter/ASE and loads clearance.	During this flight, maximum altitude and velocity were 23,334 feet and 649 knots (Mach 1.21). A maximum normal load factor of 5.22 g's was achieved. A maximum AOA of 10.73 degrees was obtained. Flight time: 0.5 hours.

#, Date, Pilot	Objectives	Comments
Flight #35 27 MAR 03 Purifoy	Continue with supersonic loads clearance & aircraft/RFCS checkout.	Maximum lateral stick input for maneuvers and the corresponding loads produced were 75-percent stick, 30 aileron-hinge moment (AILHM), and 80 percent stick, 70 percent trailing-edge-flap hinge moment (TEFHM). During this flight, maximum altitude and velocity were 21,067 feet and 643 knots (Mach 1.12). A maximum normal load factor of 4.28 g's was achieved. A maximum AOA of 11.8 degrees was obtained. Flight time: 0.3 hours.
Flight #36 27 MAR 03 Purifoy	Continue with supersonic flutter/ASE clearance.	Aborted in flight due to landing gear malfunction. Upon gear retraction, the chase pilot noted that the gear doors had not fully closed and that the right main gear had not fully retracted. The gear was extended successfully for landing. During this flight, maximum altitude and velocity were 4,151 feet and 225 knots (Mach 0.36). A maximum normal load factor of 1.4 g's was achieved. A maximum AOA of 9.83 degrees was obtained. Flight time: 0.1 hours.
Flight #37 01 APR 03 Purifoy	Continue with supersonic flutter/ASE clearance.	Pilot noted that there were significant side-force excursions on the first acceleration to test conditions. During this flight, maximum altitude and velocity were 29,991 feet and 700 knots (Mach 1.32). A maximum normal load factor of 2.95 g's was achieved. A maximum AOA of 7.86 degrees was obtained. Flight time: 0.4 hours.
Flight #38 01 APR 03 Ewers	Continue with supersonic flutter/ASE and loads clearance.	During this flight, maximum altitude and velocity were 25,345 feet and 696 knots (Mach 1.25). A maximum normal load factor of 4.09 g's was achieved. A maximum AOA of 7.32 degrees was obtained. Flight time: 0.5 hours.

#, Date, Pilot	Objectives	Comments
Flight #39 03 APR 03 Ewers	Begin supersonic OBES PID maneuvers.	During this flight, maximum altitude and velocity were 33,403 feet and 534 knots (Mach 1.2). A maximum normal load factor of 3.36 g's was achieved. A maximum AOA of 9.35 degrees was obtained. Flight time: 0.5 hours
Flight #40 03 APR 03 Ewers	Begin supersonic air data calibration maneuvers.	During this flight, maximum altitude and velocity were 29,152 feet and 654 knots (Mach 1.35). A maximum normal load factor of 3.76 g's was achieved. A maximum AOA of 7.55 degrees was obtained. Flight time: 0.7 hours.
Flight #41 03 APR 03 Purifoy	Continue with supersonic OBES PID maneuvers.	Maneuver produced 80 percent AILHM and disengaged for roll rate. Flight-deflection measurement system (FDMS) was flickering during a high-bank-angle turn. During this flight, maximum altitude and velocity were 35,509 feet and 590 knots (Mach 1.33). A maximum normal load factor of 3.65 g's was achieved. A maximum AOA of 7.95 degrees was obtained. Flight time: 0.5 hours.
Flight #42 09 APR 03 Purifoy	Continue supersonic OBES PID maneuvers and perform some intermediate test condition loads model verification maneuvers.	Left landing gear door was slow to close following takeoff. High loads were noted during OBES PID maneuvers. During this flight, maximum altitude and velocity were 29,604 feet and 565 knots (Mach 1.21). A maximum normal load factor of 5.74 g's was achieved. A maximum AOA of 8.42 degrees was obtained. Flight time: 0.5 hours.
Flight #43 09 APR 03 Purifoy	Continue supersonic OBES PID maneuvers.	During this flight, maximum altitude and velocity were 26,529 feet and 618 knots (Mach 1.26). A maximum normal load factor of 5.22 g's was achieved. A maximum AOA of 6.35 degrees was obtained. Flight time: 0.4 hours.

#, Date, Pilot	Objectives	Comments
Flight #44 09 APR 03 Purifoy	Continue with supersonic OBES PID, perform some intermediate test condition loads model verification maneuvers and some subsonic loads model verification and PID repeats.	During this flight, maximum altitude and velocity were 27,378 feet and 615 knots (Mach 1.27). A maximum normal load factor of 4.42 g's was achieved. A maximum AOA of 7.42 degrees was obtained. Flight time: 0.5 hours.
Flight #45 09 APR 03 Purifoy	Continue with supersonic OBES PID maneuvers.	During this flight, maximum altitude and velocity were 31,395 feet and 639 knots (Mach 1.32). A maximum normal load factor of 2.47 g's was achieved. A maximum AOA of 5.2 degrees was obtained. Flight time: 0.4 hours.
Flight #46 10 APR 03 Purifoy	Continue with supersonic OBES PID maneuvers.	During this flight, maximum altitude and velocity were 22,880 feet and 638 knots (Mach 1.21). A maximum normal load factor of 2.84 g's was achieved. A maximum AOA of 6.58 degrees was obtained. Flight time: 0.3 hours.
Flight #47 10 APR 03 Purifoy	Continue supersonic OBES PID maneuvers and perform some intermediate test condition loads model verification maneuvers.	Control room momentarily lost telemetry and radar tracking on the AAW aircraft. During this flight, maximum altitude and velocity were 22,225 feet and 632 knots (Mach 1.17). A maximum normal load factor of 4.6 g's was achieved. A maximum AOA of 7.82 degrees was obtained. Flight time: 0.3 hours.
Flight #48 10 APR 03 Purifoy	Perform some supersonic air data calibration maneuvers and some subsonic OBES PID repeats.	During this flight, maximum altitude and velocity were 23,419 feet and 675 knots (Mach 1.22). A maximum normal load factor of 3.65 g's was achieved. A maximum AOA of 8.15 degrees was obtained. Flight time: 0.7 hours.
Flight #49 15 APR 03 Ewers	Continue with supersonic OBES PID maneuvers and perform some subsonic OBES PID repeats.	During this flight, maximum altitude and velocity were 26,595 feet and 667 knots (Mach 1.3). A maximum normal load factor of 3.59 g's was achieved. A maximum AOA of 8.67 degrees was obtained. Flight time: 0.5 hours.

#, Date, Pilot	Objectives	Comments
Flight #50 15 APR 03 Ewers	Complete supersonic OBES PID maneuvers and supersonic loads model verification maneuvers.	During this flight, maximum altitude and velocity were 24,228 feet and 660 knots (Mach 1.12). A maximum normal load factor of 4.65 g's was achieved. A maximum AOA of 10.45 degrees was obtained. Flight time: 0.3 hours.
AAW Miscellaneous Flights		
Flight #51 25 JUN 03 Purifoy	Follow-on AAW research flight to address a few leftover items from Phase 1.	Flight time: 0.8 hours.
Flight #52 02 JUL 03 Ewers	Functional check flight.	FCF in air show configuration (normal FCS only, RFCS not engaged). Flight time: 0.8 hours.
Flight #53 15 JUL 03 Purifoy	Cross-country flight.	Edwards AFB, CA, to Colorado Springs, CO, including a fly-by of the Air Force Academy. Flight time: 1.7 hours.
Flight #54 15 JUL 03 Purifoy	Cross-country flight.	Colorado Springs to Whiteman AFB, MO. Flight time: 1.3 hours.
Flight #55 15 JUL 03 Purifoy	Cross-country flight.	Whiteman AFB to Dayton, OH, for air show at Wright-Patterson AFB. Flight time: 1.4 hours.
Flight #56 21 JUL 03 Purifoy	Cross-country flight.	Dayton to Grissom Air Reserve Base (ARB), IN. Flight time: 0.6 hours.
Flight #57 28 JUL 03 Ewers	Cross-country flight.	Grissom ARB to Oshkosh, WI, for display at Oshkosh air show. Flight time: 1.0 hour.
Flight #58 04 AUG 03 Purifoy	Cross-country flight.	Oshkosh to Salina, KS. Flight time: 1.3 hours.
Flight #59 04 AUG 03 Ewers	Cross-country flight.	Salina to Grand Junction, CO. Flight time: 1.3 hours.
Flight #60 04 AUG 03 Purifoy	Cross-country flight.	Grand Junction to Edwards AFB. Flight time: 1.3 hours.

#, Date, Pilot	Objectives	Comments
AAW Phase 2		
Flight #61 14 DEC 04 Purifoy	Functional check flight and perform subsonic deflection data maneuvers at 10,000 and 20,000 feet.	Performed FCF per 853-A1-F18AC-NFM-700.1 modified checklist. Due to problems with the transmitter, heads-up display (HUD) video was unavailable to the control room. power lever angle (PLA) position failure was generated and reset successfully during the automatic flight control system (AFCS)-Check portion of the checklist. LOLEF Hall-Effect sensor failed during the flight. Flight time: 1.2 hours.
Flight #62 14 DEC 04 Purifoy	Begin AAW Phase 2 control law development flights. Perform RFCS reversion checks, ASE, WUTs, and roll buildup.	All WUT and roll maneuvers were performed to the left. Postflight analysis was needed to clear the ¾- and full-stick roll, therefore, the build up was only carried on up to ½ stick. Flight time: 1.1 hours.
Flight #63 15 DEC 04 Purifoy	Perform RFCS reversion check, ASE, WUT, and roll buildup at 25,000 feet and Mach 1.2. Secondary objectives were to complete the roll buildup at 15,000 feet and Mach 0.95 and to perform RFCS reversion check and ASE at 10,000 feet and Mach 0.95.	All WUTs and roll maneuvers were performed to the left. Static pressure disengage occurred at the latter part of the WUT, causing a 90-percent load on the trailing-edge flap (TEF). The maneuver was repeated and completed, followed by another static pressure disengage. Rolls buildup carried out to 85- to 90-percent stick. RTB was called after Test Point (TP) 6 reversion check and ASE were successfully completed. Flight time: 0.7 hours.
Flight #64 15 DEC 04 Purifoy	Perform supersonic (Mach 1.1) RFCS reversion checks, ASE, and WUTs at 20,000 and 25,000 feet, and roll buildup. Secondary objectives were to complete the Mach 0.95 WUT and roll buildup, and to perform a level acceleration at 10,000 feet.	Roll buildup was performed up to 60-percent stick due to high loads (95 percent on the Aileron). Repeat of the ¾ stick, with full stick not cleared due to high normal acceleration on the roll. Level acceleration at 10,000 feet was performed from 0.6 to 0.9 Mach at ~3 knots/second. Flight time: 0.6 hours.

#, Date, Pilot	Objectives	Comments
Flight #65 06 JAN 05 Purifoy	Perform Mach 1.1 roll buildup at 20,000 feet, and Mach 1.2 RFCS reversion checks, ASE, WUT, and roll buildup at 15,000 feet. Secondary objectives were to complete the subsonic roll buildup at 10,000 feet and to perform a subsonic tower fly-by.	The 90-percent stick clearance resulted in 98-percent stick input causing a 106-percent load on the right rudder. Roll buildup was stopped at BINGO fuel after the ¾-stick roll. Tower fly-by was performed at about 100 feet above ground level (AGL) from 0.4 to 0.6 Mach at ~3 knots/second. Flight time: 0.5 hours.
Flight #66 06 JAN 05 Purifoy	Perform Mach 1.2 RFCS reversion check, ASE, WUT, and roll buildup at 20,000 feet, and complete the roll buildup at 15,000 feet. Secondary objectives were to complete subsonic (Mach 0.90 to 0.95) roll buildup at 10,000 feet.	Quick-turn checklist was performed at Last Chance. The LOLEF CPT was lost prior to takeoff. Sideslip noted at 60 percent stick. A tower fly-by was performed at about 100 feet AGL from Mach 0.6 to 0.9 at ~3 knots/second. Flight time: 0.6 hours.
Flight #67 06 JAN 05 Purifoy	Continue Mach 1.2 roll buildup at 20,000 feet, and complete roll buildup at 15,000 feet. Secondary objectives were to continue the Mach 0.9 roll buildup at 15,000 feet, repeat the full-stick roll, and perform Mach 0.85 RFCS Reversion check, ASE, WUT, and roll buildup at 10,000 feet.	The ¾-stick roll produced 3.6 degrees of sideslip. Quick-turn checklist was performed at Last Chance. All WUT and roll maneuvers were performed to the left, with the exception of the 60-percent-stick roll, which was performed to the right. Roll buildup was started at 90-percent stick and completed to full stick. Tower fly-by was repeated. Flight time: 0.7 hours.
Flight #68 19 JAN 05 Ewers	Perform subsonic rolls, back-to-back WUTs in 701E and RFCS, and RFCS reversion checks and ASE.	All WUT and ROLL maneuvers were performed to the left. Roll maneuver was cleared to 85-percent stick. WUTs, RFCS reversion check, and ASE completed successfully. Flight time: 0.6 hours.

#, Date, Pilot	Objectives	Comments
Flight #69 19 JAN 05 Ewers	Perform a back-to-back 701E and RFCS WUT, RFCS reversion check, and ASE.	All WUT and ROLL maneuvers were performed to the left. During back-to-back 701E and RFCS, disengage was observed after the RFCS maneuver was completed. Flight time: 0.4 hours.
Flight #70 19 JAN 05 Purifoy	Perform RFCS reversion checks, ASE, back-to-back WUT in 701E and RFCS, and roll buildup.	All roll maneuvers were performed left. Roll buildup was carried on to the ¾-stick maneuver, which was followed by an impact pressure disengage. Flight time: 0.8 hours.
Flight #71 21 JAN 05 Ewers	Perform Mach 1.3 roll buildup at 20,0000 feet, and complete Mach 1.1 roll buildup at 15,000 feet.	All roll maneuvers were performed to the left. Roll buildup was performed up to 60-percent stick, with a repeat of the ½ stick due to an impact pressure disengage during the first attempt. Flight time: 0.5 hours.
Flight #72 21 JAN 05 Ewers	Complete Mach 1.1 roll buildup at 15,000 feet and RFCS reversion check, ASE, WUT, and Mach 1.3 roll buildup at 25,000 feet.	All WUT and roll maneuvers were performed to the left. Roll buildup was started at 90-percent stick and completed at full stick. Flight time: 0.5 hours.
Flight #73 21 JAN 05 Purifoy	Complete subsonic (Mach 0.85 to 0.95) roll buildup at 5,000 and 10,000 feet, WUT and Mach 0.9 roll buildup on at 5,000 feet, and supersonic (Mach 1.1) RFCS reversion check at 10,000 feet.	All roll maneuvers were performed left. The full buildup was accomplished with ¼- to ¾-stick, 60-percent bank-to-bank maneuvers preceding the full-stick, 360-degree roll. RFCS could not be armed and engaged during reversion check. Flight time: 0.7 hours.
Flight #74 27 JAN 05 Ewers	Complete subsonic (Mach 0.95) roll buildup at 5,000 feet, continue supersonic (Mach 1.3) roll buildup at 20,000 feet, and perform RFCS reversion check, ASE, and WUT at Mach 1.1 and 10,000 feet.	All WUT and roll maneuvers were performed to the left. Roll buildup was started at a 90-percent stick, 60-degree bank-to-bank maneuver, followed by a full-stick, 60-degree bank-to-bank and a full-stick 360-degree roll. Flight time: 0.4 hours.

#, Date, Pilot	Objectives	Comments
Flight #75 27 JAN 05 Purifoy	Complete the 90-percent and full-stick left rolls at Mach 1.3 and 20,000 feet, and (rolling pullout [RPO]) buildup at 0.85 Mach and 15,000 feet.	Flight was aborted shortly after takeoff. During climb up, all landing gear doors failed to close. Chase pilot reported all three doors were wide open, that the landing gear retracted properly, and that nothing looked broken, dangling or bent. Landing gear was lowered and locked down successfully. Flight time: 0.2 hours.
Flight #76 24 FEB 05 Ewers	Perform portions of FCF profile C to check rigging of the left and right inboard and outboard leading-edge flaps, complete full-stick left roll at Mach 1.3 and 25,000 feet, complete 90-percent and full-stick left rolls at Mach 1.3 and 20,000 feet, RPO buildup at Mach 0.85 and 15,000 feet, Northrop Grumman subsonic deflection data maneuvers, and RPOs buildup at Mach 0.95 and 5,000 feet.	Maneuvers at test points 12 and 15 were performed to the left; all others were performed to the right. Some maneuvers had to be repeated. Flight time: 0.7 hours.
Flight #77 24 FEB 05 Ewers	Complete the Northrop Grumman supersonic deflection data maneuvers, perform Mach 1.2 RPO buildup at 25,000 feet, perform right roll buildup at Mach 0.85 and 15,000 feet, and RPO buildup at Mach 0.85 and 5,000 feet.	All RPO and roll maneuvers were performed to the right. The ½-stick, 4-g maneuver resulted in a disengage and 103 percent on the left aileron. Flight time: 0.5 hours.

#, Date, Pilot	Objectives	Comments
Flight #78 25 FEB 05 Ewers	Perform RPO buildup at Mach 1.2 and 15,000 feet, and at Mach 1.3 and 20,000 feet.	All RPO maneuvers were performed to the right. TP 15 RPOs: Only the ¼-stick maneuver was completed at 4 g's, all remaining were flown at 3 g's. The buildup was carried on to full-stick, with a couple maneuvers at 90-percent stick. Flight time: 0.4 hours.
Flight #79 01 MAR 05 Ewers	Complete 4-g RPO buildup at Mach 0.85 and 5,000 feet, start RPO buildup at Mach 0.85 and 10,000 feet, and Mach 1.1 roll buildup at 10,000 feet and 25,000 feet.	All RPOs were performed to the right. Some roll maneuvers were performed to the left. Roll buildup included 360-degree rolls, stopping at the 65-percent stick input that resulted in 93 percent load on the aileron. RPO buildup was performed from ¼-stick to 90 percent stick, where the left aileron reached 100 percent load. Flight time: 0.5 hours.
Flight #80 01 MAR 05 Purifoy	Perform roll buildup from Mach 1.1 to 1.3 at 20,000 feet, and Mach 1.2 at 15,000 feet; perform roll buildup at Mach 0.95 and 10,000 feet.	All roll maneuvers were performed to the right. RFCS disengaged occurred at the ¾-stick maneuver, resulting in 101-percent load on the left aileron at the recovery. This maneuver was repeated uneventfully. Flight time: 0.5 hours.
Flight #81 01 MAR 05 Ewers	Perform 4-g, Mach 1.1 RPO buildup at 15,000 feet and 20,000 feet, Mach 0.90 and 0.95 RPO at 10,000 feet, and Mach 0.85 roll buildup at 5,000 feet.	All maneuvers were performed to the right. The ¼-stick RPO maneuver was repeated at 3 g's after the 4-g maneuver resulted in disengage. The rest of the maneuvers were completed at 3 g's. Flight time: 0.5 hours.
Flight #82 02 MAR 05 Purifoy	Perform 4-g, Mach 0.9 RPO buildup at 5,000 feet and 15,000 feet, Mach 0.95 RPO at 15,000 feet, Mach 1.1 RPO at 25,000 feet, Mach 1.2 roll buildup at 25,000, Mach 0.9 roll buildup at 15,000 feet, Mach 0.85 roll buildup at 10,000 feet, and back-to-back WUTs.	All RPO and roll maneuvers were performed to the right. WUTs were performed to the left. RPO buildup began with the ¼-stick input, followed by a 45-percent-stick maneuver, then stopped after the ½-stick RPO due to high loads on the aileron. Roll buildup began at ½ stick and was ended with an 80-percent stick roll due to high loads. Flight time: 0.6 hours.

#, Date, Pilot	Objectives	Comments
Flight #83 02 MAR 05 Ewers	Perform Mach 1.1 roll buildup at 15,000 feet and 10,000 feet, Mach 1.3 roll buildup at 25,000 feet, Mach 0.95 roll buildup at 15,000 feet, RPO buildup, and back-to-back WUTs.	All RPO and roll maneuvers were performed to the right. WUTs were performed to the left. Only the ¼- and ½-stick RPO maneuvers were completed due to high loads. Flight time: 0.4 hours.
Flight #84 02 MAR 05 Purifoy	Perform Mach 0.9 roll buildup at 5,000 and 10,000 feet, Mach 0.95 roll buildup at 10,000 feet, Mach 0.85 back-to-back WUTs at 10,000 feet and 5,000 feet, Mach 1.1 and 1.3 WUTs at 25,000 feet, and Mach 0.9 WUTs at 15,000 feet.	All roll maneuvers were performed to the right, all but one of the bank-to-bank maneuvers were performed to the right, and all WUTs were performed to the left. Flight time: 0.7 hours.
Flight #85 03 MAR 05 Ewers	Perform back-to-back WUTs at several test points (Mach 1.2 and 1.3 at 20,000 feet, and Mach 1.2 at 15,000 feet), and perform Mach 0.85 wing-set rolls at 10,000 feet.	All WUTs were performed to the left. During back-to-back WUTs, RFCS maneuver resulted in disengage after the maneuver was completed. The 701E maneuver produced 101 percent load on the aileron at recovery. Flight 85 concluded with a fly-by of NASA Dryden. Flight time: 0.5 hours.
Flight #86 21 MAR 05 Purifoy	Conduct OBES maneuvers for ASE research as part of the AAW portion of FCF profile LEF check.	Maneuvers were performed at Mach 0.85 and 15,000 feet. All OBES maneuvers were initiated at a 1-g, wings-level condition. Some of the OBES sweeps for the stabilator and rudder were omitted. Performed PID doublets, Minimax curve fitting (C-F) sweeps, outboard leading-edge flap (OBLEF) sweeps, and aileron sweeps. Disengagement occurred after a symmetric collective aileron deflection maneuver. Flight time: 1.0 hour.

#, Date, Pilot	Objectives	Comments
Flight #87 21 MAR 05 Purifoy	Conduct OBES maneuvers for ASE research as part of AAW Phase 1a, and OLEF failure emulation.	All OBES maneuvers were initiated at a 1-g, wings-level condition, with the exception of the OLEF failure emulation. Some of the OBES sweeps for the stabilator and rudder were omitted. Performed Minimax C-F sweeps, OBLEF sweeps, aileron sweeps, OLEF failure emulation, wing-drop maneuver, and PID doublets. Flight time: 0.8 hours.
Flight #88 29 MAR 05 Ewers	The objectives of this flight were part of the RFCS secondary control law design overlay performed as added research to the AAW Phase 2 primary set of control laws. Specific objectives included RFCS reversion checks, ASE, WUTs, and roll buildups.	All WUTs were performed to the left. Rolls were performed to the left and right. Flight time: 0.5 hours.
Flight #89 29 MAR 05 Ewers	Continue the RFCS secondary control law design overlay. Perform ASE, WUT, and roll buildup.	The WUT was performed to the left. Rolls were performed to the left and right. Flight time: 0.5 hours.
Flight #90 29 MAR 05 Purifoy	Continue the RFCS secondary control law design overlay. Continue Mach 1.2 to 1.3 roll buildup at 20,000 feet, and perform ASE, WUT, and roll buildup at Mach 1.2 and 15,000 feet.	The WUT was performed to the left. Rolls were performed to the left and right. Flight time: 0.5 hours.

#, Date, Pilot	Objectives	Comments
Flight #91 29 MAR 05 Purifoy	Continue the RFCS secondary control law design overlay. Repeat back-to-back WUTs at Mach 0.95 and 10,000 feet, complete Mach 1.3 roll buildup at 20,000 feet, continue Mach 1.2 roll buildup at 15,000 feet, perform ASE, WUT, and roll buildup at Mach 1.1 and 25,000 feet, and perform ASE and WUT at Mach 0.95 and 15,000 feet.	All WUTs were performed to the left. Rolls were performed to the left and right. During the first two WUTs, the RFCS disengaged prior to completing the maneuver. Flight time: 0.5 hours.
Flight #92 31 MAR 05 Purifoy	Continue the RFCS secondary control law design overlay. Perform subsonic ASE, WUTs, and roll buildup, and complete the supersonic roll buildup.	All WUTs were performed to the left. Rolls were performed to the left and to the right. Flight time: 0.7 hours.
Flight #93 31 MAR 05 Purifoy	Continue the RFCS secondary control law design overlay. Perform supersonic ASE, WUT, and roll buildup, and repeat back-to-back WUTs at Mach 0.95 and 10,000 feet.	All WUTs and roll maneuvers were performed to the left. Purifoy's last NASA research flight. Flight time: 0.5 hours.
Flight #94 31 MAR 05 Ewers	Continue the RFCS secondary control law design overlay. Perform supersonic roll buildup, supersonic RPO buildup, and supersonic back-to-back WUTs.	All WUT and Roll maneuvers were performed to the left. All RPOs were performed to the right. Flight time: 0.4 hours.

#, Date, Pilot	Objectives	Comments
Flight #95 31 MAR 05 Ewers	Complete the RFCS secondary control law design overlay. Perform a repeat of the ¾- and full-stick rolls at Mach 0.95 and 5,000 feet, and supersonic RPO buildup.	Final AAW Phase 2 research flight. Roll maneuvers were performed to the left and right. All RPOs were performed to the right. Flight time: 0.5 hours.
AAW Follow-on Flights		
Flight #96 11 APR 05 Ewers	Collect wing-deflection data through a predetermined flight profile at 20,000 feet and Mach 0.9. Secondary objectives were to perform a series of Mach 0.85 push-over-pull-ups (POPUs) at 10,000 and 20,000 feet.	The deflection-data pattern and POPUs were performed successfully, and the subsonic series was performed twice. Flight time: 0.9 hours.

Aircraft Specifications

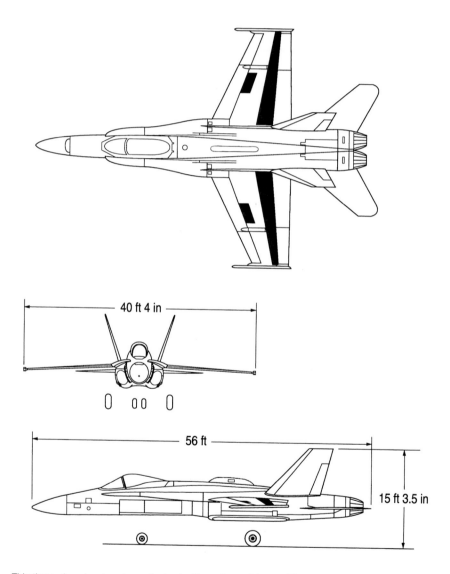

This three-view drawing shows the basic dimensions of the modified F-18 used in the AAW flight research program. (NASA)

APPENDIX 3:
AAW Configuration Management Plan

This document sets forth the configuration management and control procedures and policies for development and flight test of the AAW flight research aircraft. As specified by the AAW Annex to the WL/NASA DFRC/AFFTC Flight Research Memorandum of Understanding, the AAW Program is a joint USAF/NASA program wherein the Wright Laboratory's Flight Dynamics Directorate will modify a NASA aircraft and the NASA Dryden Flight Research Center will flight test the aircraft. The WL/FI will serve as overall program manager and will contract to modify the aircraft. The NASA DFRC will serve as the Responsible Test Organization and will have flight safety responsibility.

Because of this split of authority in the program it is necessary to be very specific as to the required participation of each organization to include how that participation will change as the program progresses.

CONFIGURATION CONTROL BOARD

The WL/FI-3 shall serve as the AAW Configuration Control Board (CCB) Chairman as authorized by the commander, Wright Laboratory (WL/CC). The configuration control board shall consist of the following:
- CCB Chairman/WL/FI-3
- AAW Program Manager/WL/FIBV
- AAW IPT Chairman/WL/FIBV
- AAW Flight Project Manager/NASA DFRC
- AAW AFFTC Representative/AFFTC

The CCB Chairman shall approve each major program segment and any out-of-scope changes to the AAW program upon recommendation by the board members who shall receive appropriate information from the various AAW boards and committees that have made technical determinations about program progress. These recommendations shall assure that expenditure of funds will achieve the technical goals with appropriate emphasis on safety of flight. (Since the AAW aircraft belongs to NASA DFRC and they have flight safety authority, clearance to fly the AAW aircraft shall be issued by NASA.)

ACTIVE AEROELASTIC WING RESEARCH BOARD (AAWRB)

The Research Board shall serve in an executive advisory capacity to assure that the AAW program maintains appropriate research and development content. The board is comprised as follows:
- AAW Program Manager/WL/FIBV, Chairman
- AAW Chief Engineer/WL/FIBV
- Dryden Chief Aeroelastician/NASA DFRC
- Langley Chief Aeroelastician/NASA LaRC
- NAA AAW Chief Aeroelastician/Boeing Corp.
- MDA AAW Chief Aeroelastician/McDonnell Douglas Co.
- AFFTC AAW Chief Aeroelastician/ AFFTC
- WL Integration Engineer/ WL
- Dryden Flight Controls Engineer/ NASA DFRC
- WL Flight Controls Engineer/ WL
- AAW Consultant Aeroelastician/ SwRI

PHYSICAL CONFIGURATION CONTROL BOARD (PCCB)
for Design and Fabrication

The AAW Physical Configuration Control Board (PCCB) for design and fabrication shall be responsible for reviewing all data presented at the Preliminary Design Review (PDR) and Critical Design Review (CDR) and make recommendations to the CCB for approval to proceed to the subsequent program segment. It also will perform the Physical Configuration Inspection (PCI) and make recommendation to transfer configuration management authority to NASA DFRC. The PCCB shall also track and assure proper documentation of test aircraft physical configuration changes. The PCCB during design and fabrication shall consist of the following:
- AAW Program Manager, Chairman/WL/FIBV
- AAW Chief Engineer, Configuration Manager/WL/FIBV
- DFRC AAW Flight Project Manager (RTO)/ NASA
- IMR Team Chairman/ ASC
- DFRC AAW Chief Engineer/ NASA
- Integration Engineer/ WL/FII
- Flight Controls Engineer/ WL/FIG

- Structures Engineer/ WL/FIB
- Aerodynamics Engineer/ WL/FIM
- AAW Prime Contractor Program Manager/ MDA
- AAW Sub Contractor Program Manager/ RI
- DFRC Operations Engineer/ NASA
- LaRC Structures Technology Engineer/ NASA
- DFRC Flight Controls Engineer/ NASA
- DFRC AAW Project Pilot/ NASA

After the PCI the modified aircraft will be turned over to NASA DFRC. Physical configuration control shall then be the responsibility of NASA DFRC and the PCCB shall be reformulated as described in the following section.

PHYSICAL CONFIGURATION CONTROL BOARD (PCCB) for Flight Test

The Chairman and Members of the PCCB shall change after PCI, before the Flight Readiness Review (FRR). Chaired by the RTO, its function will likewise change to provide on-site configuration management during the flight test phase to deal with the flight-to-flight configuration changes. The RTO shall have approval authority for all such configuration changes except:

1. Those changes that significantly effect technology objectives and program schedule: these should be reported to the WL AAW Program Office. (See flow chart.)
2. Those changes that are out-of-scope of the WL AAW Program Office contract: these shall be submitted to the CCB for approval. (See flow chart.)

The WL budget anticipates some modification, mainly software, will be required during the flight test phase. Membership on the PCCB during flight test shall be as follows: (All members are from NASA DFRC unless otherwise indicated.)

1. Flight Project Manager (RTO), Chairman
2. Chief Engineer, alternate chairman
3. Operations Engineer, alternate chairman
4. CCB Administrator
5. Systems Engineer
6. Instrumentation Engineer
7. Project Pilot
8. Crew Chief
9. Avionics Crew Chief
10. Test Information Engineer

11. Simulation Engineer
12. Controls Engineer
13. Structural Dynamics Engineer
14. Structures Engineer
15. Flight Test Engineer
16. Principal Investigators
17. WL AAW Representative
18. Contractor Program Representatives
    » Boeing St. Louis Modifications Engineer
    » Boeing St. Louis Software Engineer
    » Boeing Seal Beach Control Laws Engineer

The PCCB for flight test will follow NASA DFRC procedures except out-of-scope changes, which shall be approved by the CCB.

CONFIGURATION CONTROL PROCEDURES

Preliminary Design: During this phase the contractor will translate conceptual designs into a preliminary design that applies to the specific AAW flight research demonstration article including layout drawings, aerodynamic performance estimates, structural and subsystem modifications, preliminary sizing, establish overall software requirements, start design simulations, etc. During this phase the contractor(s) will be changing the design frequently as it evolves. *No formal configuration control* is necessary or desired except that the contractors must keep the government informed on their progress and report any problems of meeting objectives. If any problems are encountered that prevent the contractors from meeting objectives within the resources available during the planned time period, they should notify the AAW Program Manager immediately.

Detailed Design: During this phase the contractors shall develop design specifications for the final design including detailed drawings for manufacturing, specifications for all subsystems, final design simulations, performance estimates related to flight test conditions, start hardware in the loop simulations, order and receive all parts and subsystems required for manufacturing, prepare testbed aircraft for modification, etc. During this phase *no formal configuration control* is necessary, however, any deviations from the preliminary design presented at the Preliminary Design Review (PDR) shall be reported immediately to the AAW Program Manager.

Fabrication/Modification: During this phase the modification is fabricated and installed on the testbed aircraft. *Formal hardware configuration control* will be instituted after Critical Design Review (CDR) or at the start of this phase. The procedures to be followed are described below.

Physical Configuration Inspection (PCI): At completion of fabrication/modification the AAW Aircraft will be inspected by the government for compliance with modification standards and returned to its original configuration for ferry to NASA DFRC. After arrival at NASA DFRC the AAW Aircraft will be returned to flight research configuration and a formal PCI will be performed by the government. After formal approval of the PCI *formal software configuration control* will be instituted. (Maybe this should be after V & V.)

CONFIGURATION CHANGE CLASSIFICATION

Class I Changes:
- Affects baseline design or function
- Impact cost or schedule
- Outside contract scope
- Affects GFE requirements
- Affects Safety of Flight
- Affects delivered hardware or software
- Requires Government approval

Class II Changes:
- All others
- Requires Government approval only if initiated by the Government or occurs during flight test

CHANGE CONTROL PROCEDURES

Changes can be identified by either the contractor or the government. For Class I changes the contractor shall submit an Engineering Change Request (ECR) in accordance with the changes clause of the contract. The government will convene a PCCB review. If the change is out-of-scope it will be submitted to the CCB for approval. The Procurement Contracting Officer (PCO) will direct the contractor to institute the change. The contractor will document all Class I changes formally and all Class II changes can be reported in a monthly status report. All changes will be documented by the contractor in accordance with NASA DFRC procedures including the updating of test aircraft manuals and logs.

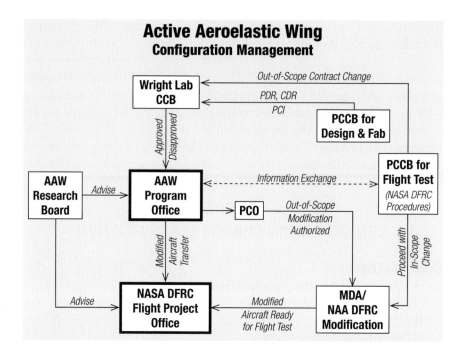

ACTIVE AEROELASTIC WING PROGRAM BOARD MEMBERS

CONFIGURATION CONTROL BOARD

WL/CC or designee, CCB Chairman/WL Dr. Donald Paul
AAW Program Manager/IPT Chairman/WL Mr. Ed Pendleton
AAW Flight Project Manager/NASA DFRC Mr. Denis Bessette
AAW AFFTC Representative/AFFTC Mr. Robert Evans

ACTIVE AEROELASTIC WING RESEARCH BOARD (AAWRB)

AAW Program Manager, Chairman/WL/FIBV: Mr. Ed Pendleton
AAW Chief Engineer/WL/FIBV: Mr. Pete Flick
Dryden Chief Aeroelastician/NASA DFRC: Mr. Mike DeAngelis
Langley Chief Aeroelastician/NASA LaRC: Mr. Boyd Perry
NAA AAW Chief Aeroelastician/Boeing Corp.: Mr. Gerald Miller
MDA AAW Chief Aeroelastician/McDonnell Douglas: Mr. Rudy Yurkovich
AFFTC AAW Chief Aeroelastician/ AFFTC: Mr. Tracy Redd
WL Integration Engineer/ WL/FII: Mr. Ken Bonnema
Dryden Flight Controls Engineer/ NASA DFRC: _____
WL Flight Controls Engineer/ WL: Mr. Finley Barfield
AAW Consultant Aeroelastician/ SwRI: Dr. Kenneth Griffin

PHYSICAL CONFIGURATION CONTROL BOARD
(PCCB) for Design and Fabrication
AAW Program Manager, Chairman/WL/FIBV: Mr. Ed Pendleton
AAW Chief Engineer, Configuration Manager/WL/FIBV: Mr. Pete Flick
AAW Flight Project Manager/ NASA DFRC (RTO): Mr. Denis Bessette
IMR Team Chairman/ ASC: Mr. Robert Moore
Chief Engineer/ NASA DFRC: Mr. Dave Voracek
Integration Engineer/ WL/FII: Mr. Ken Bonnema
Flight Controls Engineer/ WL/FIG: Mr. Finley Barfield
Structures Engineer/ WL/FIB: Dr. Ray Kolonay
Aerodynamics Engineer/ WL/FIM: Capt Brian Parker
AAW Prime Contractor Program Manager/ MDA: Mr. Pete Fields
AAW Sub Contractor Program Manager/NAA Boeing: Dr. Robert Schwanz
DFRC Operations Engineer/ NASA: _____
LaRC Structures Technology Engineer/ NASA: Mr. Boyd Perry
DFRC Flight Controls Engineer/ NASA: _____
DFRC AAW Project Pilot/ NASA: Mr. Jim Smolka

PHYSICAL CONFIGURATION CONTROL BOARD (PCCB) for Flight Test
All members are from NASA DFRC unless otherwise indicated.
1. Flight Project Manager (RTO), Chairman
2. Chief Engineer, alternate chairman
3. Operations Engineer, alternate chairman
4. CCB Administrator
5. Systems Engineer
6. Instrumentation Engineer
7. Project Pilot
8. Crew Chief
9. Avionics Crew Chief
10. Test Information Engineer
11. Simulation Engineer
12. Controls Engineer
13. Structural Dynamics Engineer
14. Structures Engineer
15. Flight Test Engineer
16. Principal Investigators
17. WL AAW Representative
18. Contractor Program Representatives
    » Boeing St. Louis Modifications Engineer
    » Boeing St. Louis Software Engineer
    » Boeing Seal Beach Control Laws Engineer

APPENDIX 4:
Key Technical Reports

Allen, Michael J., and Ryan P. Dibley. "Modeling Aircraft Wing Loads from Flight Data Using Neural Networks." NASA TM-2003-212032 (September 2003).

Allen, Michael J., Andrew M. Lizotte, Ryan P. Dibley, and Robert Clarke. "Loads Model Development and Analysis for the F/A-18 Active Aeroelastic Wing Airplane." NASA TM-2005-213663 (March 2005).

Anderson, Robert A. "Concept Layout for LE Flap System Modifications for the Active Aeroelastic Wing Program." McDonnell Douglas Aerospace (June 1997).

Anderson, Robert A. "Design Requirements for LE Flap System Modifications for the Active Aeroelastic Wing Program." McDonnell Douglas Aerospace (June 1997).

Anderson, Robert A., Eric Reichenbach, Ron Hess, Kenneth Griffin, Peter Flick, Dana Purifoy, Denis Bessette, Larry Myers, Dave Voracek, John Baca, Marty Brenner, Bill Lokos, Jim Guffey, Dave Riley, and Edmund Pendleton. "Summary of Lessons Learned from the Active Aeroelastic Wing Flight Research Program." U.S. Industry Aerospace Flutter and Dynamics Council Meeting, Atlanta, GA (May 2005).

Baldelli, Dario H., Richard Lind, and Martin Brenner. "Nonlinear Aeroelastic/ Aeroservoelastic Modeling by Block-Oriented Identification." *Journal of Guidance, Control, and Dynamics* 28, no. 5 (September–October 2005): pp. 1,056–1,064.

Boehm, Ben, Peter Flick, Brian Sanders, Chris Pettit, Eric Reichenbach, and Scott Zillmer. "Static Aeroelastic Response Predictions of the Active Aeroelastic Wing (AAW) Flight Research Vehicle." Paper 2001-1372, AIAA/ ASME/ASCE/AHS/ASC Structures, Structural Dynamics, and Materials Conference, Seattle, WA (April 2000).

Brenner, Martin J. "Aeroservoelastic Uncertainty Model Identification from Flight Data." NASA-TM-2001-210397 (July 2001).

Brenner, Martin J., and Dale Groutage. "Nonstationary Dynamics Data Analysis with Wavelet-SVD Filtering." NASA TM-2001-210391 (April 2001).

Brenner, Martin J., and Chad Prazenica. "Aeroelastic Flight Data Analysis with the Hilbert-Huang Algorithm." NASA TM-2006-213665 (January 2006).

Brenner, Martin J., and Richard J. Prazenica. "Aeroservoelastic Model Validation and Test Data Analysis of the F/A-18 Active Aeroelastic Wing." NASA TM-2003-212021 (April 2003).

Buttrill, Carey S., and Jacob A. Houck. "Hot-Bench Simulation of the Active Flexible Wing Wind-Tunnel Model." NASA TM-102758 (November 1990).

Clarke, Robert, Michael J. Allen, Ryan P. Dibley, Joseph Gera, and John Hodgkinson. "Flight Test of the F/A-18 Active Aeroelastic Wing Airplane." NASA TM-2005-213664 (August 2005).

Dibley, Ryan P., Michael J. Allen, Robert Clarke, Joseph Gera, and John Hodgkinson. "Development and Testing of Control Laws for the Active Aeroelastic Wing Program." NASA TM-2005-213666 (December 2005).

Diebler, Corey G., and Stephen B. Cumming. "Active Aeroelastic Wing Aerodynamic Model Development and Validation for a Modified F/A-18A Airplane." NASA TM-2005-213668 (November 2005).

Field, Peter B., Eric Y. Reichenbach, Robert C. Anderson, Oliver K. Hall, Ronald K. Hess, Steven H. Goldthorpe, Nicholas J. Lapointe, and Thomas C. Nurczyk. "The Active Aeroelastic Wing (AAW) Flight Research Program, the X-53—Final Report." AFRL-VA-WP-TR-2005-3082, Air Force Research Laboratory, Air Vehicles Directorate (August 2005).

Flick, Peter M., and Michael H. Love. "The Impact of Active Aeroelastic Wing Technology on Conceptual Aircraft Design." *Structural Aspects of Flexible Aircraft Control*, RTO-MP-036, NATO Research and Technology Organization, presented at the Specialist's Meeting of the RTO Applied Vehicle Technology Panel, Ottawa, Canada (October 1999).

Griffin, Kenneth E. "Design Methodology for Control Force Predictions of Active Aeroelastic Wings." AFRL/VA Contractor Report (March 2006).

Heeg, Jennifer. "Control Surface Interaction Effects of the Active Aeroelastic Wing Wind Tunnel Model." Paper 2006-2185, 47th AIAA/ASME/ASCE/AHS/ASC Structures, Structural Dynamics, and Materials Conference, Newport, RI (May 2006).

Heeg, Jennifer, Charles V. Spain, James R. Florance, Carol D. Wiesemen, Thomas G. Ivanco, Joshua A. DeMoss, Walter A. Silva, Andrew Panetta, Peter Lively, and Vic Tumwa. "Experimental Results from the Active Aeroelastic Wing Wind Tunnel Test Program." AIAA 2005-2234, presented at the 46th AIAA/ASME/ASCE/AHS/ASC Structures, Structural Dynamics & Materials Conference, Austin, TX (April 2005).

Kehoe, Michael W., and Lawrence C. Freudinger. "Aircraft Ground Vibration Testing at the NASA Dryden Research Facility—1993." NASA TM-104275 (April 1994).

Kukreja, Sunil L., and Martin J. Brenner. "Nonlinear Aeroelastic System Identification with Application to Experimental Data." *Journal of Guidance, Control, and Dynamics* 29, no. 2 (March–April 2006): pp. 374–381.

Lizotte, Andrew M., and Michael J. Allen. "Twist Model Development and Results from the Active Aeroelastic Wing F/A-18 Aircraft." NASA TM-2005-212861 (March 2005).

Lizotte, Andrew M., and William A. Lokos. "Deflection-Based Structural Loads Estimation From the Active Aeroelastic Wing F/A-18 Aircraft." NASA TM-2005-212871 (May 2005).

Lokos, William A., Andrew M. Lizotte, Ned J. Lindsley, and Rick Stauf. "Shock Location Dominated Transonic Flight Loads on the Active Aeroelastic Wing." NASA TM-2005-213667 (December 2005).

Lokos, William A., Candida D. Olney, Tony Chen, Natalie D. Crawford, Rick Stauf, and Eric Y. Reichenbach. "Strain-Gage Loads Calibration Testing of the Active Aeroelastic Wing F/A-18 Aircraft." NASA TM-2002-210726 (June 2002).

Lokos, William A., Candida D. Olney, Natalie D. Crawford, Rick Stauf, and Erich Y. Reichenbach. "Wing Torsional Stiffness Tests of the Active Aeroelastic Wing F/A-18 Airplane." NASA TM-2002-210723 (May 2002).

Lokos, William A., and Rick Stauf. "Strain-Gage Loads Calibration Parametric Study." NASA TM-2004-212853 (August 2004).

Miller, Gerald D. "Active Flexible Wing (AFW) Technology." TR-87-3096, Air Force Wright Aeronautical Laboratories (February 1988).

Miller, Gerald D. "An Active Flexible Wing Multi-Disciplinary Design Optimization Method." Paper 94-4412-CP, *Proceedings of the 5th AIAA Symposium on Multidisciplinary Analysis and Optimization*, AIAA 94-4412-CP (September 1994).

Miller, Gerald D. "AFW Design Methodology Study." Rockwell-Aerospace Report No. NA 94-1731 (December 1994).

Moes, Timothy R., Gregory K. Noffz, and Kenneth W. Iliff. "Results From F-18B Stability and Control Parameter Estimation Flight Tests at High Dynamic Pressures." NASA TP-2000-209033 (November 2000).

Noll, Thomas E., Boyd Perry III, Sherwood H. Tiffany, Stanley R. Cole, Carey S. Buttrill, William M. Adams Jr., Jacob A. Houck, S. Srinathkumar, Vivek Mukhopadhyay, Anthony S. Pototzky, Jennifer Heeg, Sandra M. McGraw, Gerald D. Miller, Rosemary Ryan, Michael Brosnan, James Haverty, and Martin Klepl. "Aeroservoelastic Wind-Tunnel Investigations Using the Active Flexible Wing Model—Status and Recent Accomplishments." NASA TM-101570 (1989).

Norris, M., and Gerald D. Miller. "AFW Technology Assessment." Lockheed Aeronautical Systems Company and Rockwell-Aerospace Report No. NA 94-1740 (December 1994).

Olney, Candida D., Heather Hillebrandt, and Eric Y. Reichenbach. "An Evaluation Technique for an F/A-18 Aircraft Loads Model Using F/A-18 Systems Research Aircraft Flight Data." NASA TM-2000-209028 (July 2000).

Pendleton, Edmund W. "Active Aeroelastic Wing." *Technology Horizons* 1, no. 2 (June 2000): pp. 27–28.

Pendleton, Edmund W. "Back to the Future: How Active Aeroelastic Wings are a Return to Aviation's Beginnings and a Small Step to Future Bird-like Wings." Keynote Paper, NATO RTO Meeting on Active Control Technology for Enhanced Performance Operational Capabilities of Military Aircraft, Land Vehicles, and Sea Vehicles, Braunschweig, Germany (May 2000).

Pendleton, Edmund W., Denis Bessette, Peter B. Field, Gerald D. Miller, and Kenneth E. Griffin. "The Active Aeroelastic Wing Flight Research Program." Paper 98-1972, 39th AIAA Structures, Structural Dynamics, and Materials Conference, Long Beach, CA (April 1998).

Pendleton, Edmund W., Kenneth Griffin, Michael Kehoe, and Boyd Perry. "A Flight Research Program for Active Aeroelastic Wing Technology: Technical Program and Model Analytical Development." Paper 96-1574, 37th AIAA Structures, Structural Dynamics, and Materials Conference, Salt Lake City, UT (April 1996).

Pendleton, Edmund W., Mark Lee, and Lee Wasserman. "Application of Active Flexible Wing Technology to the Agile Falcon." *Journal of Aircraft* 29, no. 3 (May–June 1992).

Pendleton, Edmund W., David Voracek, Eric Reichenbach, and Kenneth Griffin. "The X-53: A Summary of the Active Aeroelastic Wing Flight Research Program." AIAA-2007-1855, 48th AIAA/ASME/ASCE/AHS/ASC Structures, Structural Dynamics, and Materials Conference, Honolulu, HI (April 2007).

Perry, Boyd, Stanley R. Cole, Gerald D. Miller. "A Summary of an Active Flexible Wing Program." *Journal of Aircraft* 32, no. 1 (January–February 1995).

Prazenica, Richard J., Martin J. Brenner, and Richard Lind. "Nonlinear System Identification for the F/A-18 Active Aeroelastic Wing." AIAA SDM, Palm Springs, CA (April 2004).

Regenie, Victoria A., Michael Earls, Jeanette Le, and Michael Thompson. "Experience with Ada on the F-18 High Alpha Research Vehicle Flight Test Program." NASA TM-104259 (October 1992).

Regenie, Victoria A., Donald Gatlin, Robert Kempel, and Neil Matheny. "The F-18 High Alpha Research Vehicle: A High Angle of Attack Research Testbed Aircraft." NASA TM-104253 (September 1992).

Reichenbach, Eric Y. "Development and Validation of F/A-18 Wing Preliminary Design Finite Element Model." McDonnell Douglas (April, 1997).

Voracek, David, Ed Pendleton, Eric Reichenbach, Kenneth Griffin, and Leslie Welch. "The Active Aeroelastic Wing Flight Research Program: Summary of Technical Program & Phase I Flight Research." NATO RTO AVT Applied Vehicle Technology Meeting on Novel Vehicle Concepts and Emerging Vehicle Technologies, Brussels, Belgium (April 2003).

Wieseman, Carol D., Walter A. Silva, Charles V. Spain, and Jennifer Heeg. "Transonic-Small-Disturbance and Linear Analyses for the Active Aeroelastic Wing Program." 46th AIAA/ASME/ASCE/AHS/ASC Structures, Structural Dynamics & Materials Conference, Austin, TX (April 2005).

Young, Peter, and Ronald J. Patton. "Comparison Test Signals for Aircraft Frequency Domain Identification." *AIAA Journal of Guidance, Control, and Dynamics* 13, no. 3 (May–June 1990).

Yurkovich, Rudy. "Optimum Wing Shape for an AFW." Paper 95-1220-CP, 36th AIAA Structures, Structural Dynamics, and Materials Conference, New Orleans, LA (April 1995).

Zillmer, Scott. "Integrated Multidisciplinary Optimization for Aeroelastic Wing Design." Air Force Wright Laboratory TR-97-3087 (August 1997).

Zillmer, Scott. "Integrated Structure/Maneuver Design Procedure for Active Aeroelastic Wings, User's Manual." Air Force Wright Laboratory TR-97-3037 (March 1997).

Bibliography

Reports, Papers, Articles, and Presentations

Achondo, Ivan A. "Active Aeroelastic Wing (AAW) NASA F/A-18 #853 Phase II Flight Report: Flights 61-67." NASA (January 2005).

Anderson, Bob, Eric Reichenbach, Ron Hess, Ken Griffin, Pete Flick, Dana Purifoy, Denis Bessette, Larry Myers, Dave Voracek, John Baca, Marty Brenner, Bill Lokos, Jim Guffey, Dave Riley, and Ed Pendleton. "Summary of Lessons Learned from the Active Aeroelastic Wing Flight Research Program." draft copy (May 2005).

Buttrill, Carey S., and Jacob A. Houck. "Hot-Bench Simulation of the Active Flexible Wing Wind-Tunnel Model." NASA TM-102758 (November 1990).

Carter, John, and Mark Stephenson. "Initial Flight Test of the Production Support Flight Control Computers at NASA Dryden Flight Research Center." NASA TM-1999-206581 (August 1999).

Clarke, Robert, Michael J. Allen, Ryan P. Dibley, Joseph Gera, and John Hodgkinson. "Flight Test of the F/A-18 Active Aeroelastic Wing Airplane." NASA TM-2005-213664 (August 2005).

Cole, Stanley R., Thomas E. Noll, and Boyd Perry III. "Transonic Dynamics Tunnel Aeroelastic Testing in Support of Aircraft Development." *Journal of Aircraft* 40, no. 5, (September–October 2003).

Crawford, Natalie. "AAW Wing Torsional Stiffness Test Report with Preliminary Findings." NASA AAW-2001-010 (April 2001).

Davies, Clifton, Marc Stelmack, Scott Zink, Antonio De La Garza, and Pete Flick. "High Fidelity MDO Process Development and Application to Fighter Strike Conceptual Design." AIAA-2012-5490, 12th AIAA Aviation

Technology, Integration, and Operations Conference, Indianapolis, IN (September 2012).

Dibley, Ryan P., Michael J. Allen, Robert Clarke, Joseph Gera, and John Hodgkinson. "Development and Testing of Control Laws for the Active Aeroelastic Wing Program." NASA TM-2005-213666 (December 2005).

Diebler, Corey G., and Stephen B. Cumming. "Active Aeroelastic Wing Aerodynamic Model Development and Validation for a Modified F/A-18A Airplane." NASA TM-2005-213668 (November 2005).

Field, Peter B., Eric Y. Reichenbach, Robert C. Anderson, Oliver K. Hall, Ronald K. Hess, Steven H. Goldthorpe, Nicholas J. Lapointe, and Thomas C. Nurczyk. "The Active Aeroelastic Wing (AAW) Flight Research Program, the X-53—Final Report." AFRL-VA-WP-TR-2005-3082, Air Force Research Laboratory, Air Vehicles Directorate (August 2005).

Flick, Peter M., and Michael H. Love. "The Impact of Active Aeroelastic Wing Technology on Conceptual Aircraft Design." *Structural Aspects of Flexible Aircraft Control*, RTO-MP-036, NATO Research and Technology Organization, presented at the Specialist's Meeting of the RTO Applied Vehicle Technology Panel, Ottawa, Canada (October 1999).

Hansen, Curt, Jacob Schaefer, John J. Burken, Marcus Johnson, and Nhan Nguyen. "Handling Qualities Evaluations of Low Complexity Model Reference Adaptive Controllers for Reduced Pitch and Roll Damping Scenarios." AIAA Guidance, Navigation, and Control Conference (August 2011).

Harris, Terry M., and Lawrence J. Huttsell. "Aeroelasticity Research at Wright-Patterson Air Force Base (Wright Field) from 1953–1993." *Journal of Aircraft* 40, no. 5 (September–October 2003).

Heeg, Jennifer, Charles V. Spain, James R. Florance, Carol D. Wiesemen, Thomas G. Ivanco, Joshua A. DeMoss, Walter A. Silva, Andrew Panetta, Peter Lively, and Vic Tumwa. "Experimental Results from the Active Aeroelastic Wing Wind Tunnel Test Program." AIAA 2005-2234, presented at the 46th AIAA/ASME/ASCE/AHS/ASC Structures, Structural Dynamics & Materials Conference, Austin, TX (April 2005).

Heeg, Jennifer, Charles V. Spain, and J.A. Rivera. "Wind Tunnel to Atmospheric Mapping for Static Aeroelastic Scaling." AIAA 2004-2044, presented at the 45th AIAA/ASME/ASCE/AHS/ASC Structures, Structural Dynamics and Materials Conference, Palm Springs, CA (April 2004).

Lizotte, Andrew M., and William A. Lokos. "Deflection-Based Aircraft Structural Loads Estimation with Comparison to Flight." AIAA-2005-2016, presented at the AIAA/ASME/ASCE/AHS/ASC Structures, Structural Dynamics & Materials Conference, Austin, TX (April 2005).

Lokos, William A. "Test Plan for the F-18 AAW (TN853) Wing Strain Gage Loads Calibration Test." NASA Dryden Flight Research Center (March 2001).

Lokos, William A., Candida D. Olney, Natalie D. Crawford, Rick Stauf, and Erich Y. Reichenbach. "Wing Torsional Stiffness Tests of the Active Aeroelastic Wing F/A-18 Airplane." NASA TM-2002-210723 (May 2002).

Pendleton, Edmund. "Back to the Future: How Active Aeroelastic Wings are a Return to Aviation's Beginnings and a Small Step to Future Bird-Like Wings." NATO RTO AVT Symposium on Active Control Technology for Enhanced Performance Operational Capabilities of Military Aircraft, Land Vehicles and Sea Vehicles, Braunschweig, Germany (May 2000).

Pendleton, Edmund, Dave Voracek, Eric Reichenbach, and Kenneth Griffin. "The X-53: A Summary of the Active Aeroelastic Wing Flight Research Program." AIAA-2007-1855, 48th AIAA/ASME/ASCE/AHS/ASC Structures, Structural Dynamics, and Materials Conference, Honolulu, HI (April 2007).

Perry, Boyd, Stanley R. Cole, and Gerald D. Miller. "Summary of an Active Flexible Wing Program." *Journal of Aircraft* 32, no. 1 (January–February 1995).

Reichenbach, Eric. "Explanation of AAW Wing Torsional Stiffness Test Results and Impact on Achieving AAW Flight Research Objectives." Provided by Dave Voracek, NASA Dryden Flight Research Center, from personal files (November 2001).

Tulinius, Jan. "Active Flexible Wing Aircraft Control System." U.S. Patent 5,082,207, filed July 16, 1990, issued January 21, 1992.

Welch, Leslie M. "Active Aeroelastic Wing (AAW) NASA F/A-18 #853 Flight Report: Flights 1-5." NASA (November 2002).

Welch, Leslie M. "Active Aeroelastic Wing (AAW) NASA F/A-18 #853 Flight Report: Flights 8-11." NASA (January 2003).

Welch, Leslie M. "Active Aeroelastic Wing (AAW) NASA F/A-18 #853 Flight Report: Flights 17-25." NASA (March 2003).

White, S.L. "Active Flexible Wing Technology Demonstration: A Proposal in Response to NASA Research Announcement NRA-94-0A-02—Advanced Concepts for Aeronautics." Rockwell International, North American Aircraft Division (February 25, 1994).

Zillmer, Scott. "Integrated Maneuver Load Control (MLC) for Active Flexible Wing (AFW) Design—Final Briefing." Boeing North American Aircraft Division (May 21, 1997).

Books and Monographs

Hallion, Richard P. *Test Pilots: The Frontiersmen of Flight* (Washington, DC: Smithsonian Institution Press, 1988).

Kemp, Martin. *Leonardo da Vinci, the Marvellous Works of Nature and Man* (Cambridge, MA: Harvard University Press, 1981).

Other Resources

Bessette, Denis E. Memo re: "Assignment of Dryden Aircraft to the Active Aeroelastic Wing (AAW) Program." Provided by Dave Voracek, NASA Dryden Flight Research Center, from personal files (1995).

Brenner, Marty, William Lokos, John Carter, and David F. Voracek. "Objectives and Requirements Document—Active Aeroelastic Wing (AAW)." AAW-840-ORD-v1.0, NASA Dryden Flight Research Center (July 1998).

Brown, Alan. "AAW makes first flight." *The X-Press* 44, no. 4 (November 2002).

Brown, Alan. "AAW notes from video interview." From personal files of Alan Brown (January 12, 2004).

Gelzer, Christian, and Jay Levine. "Re-Wright: Wing design of the future borrows from original flyer." *The X-Press*, Special Active Aeroelastic Wing Edition (December 17, 2003).

Jordan, Holly. "Active Aeroelastic Wing flight research vehicle receives X-53 designation." *http://www.wpafb.af.mil/news/story.asp?id=123035661*, December 11, 2006.

Levine, Jay. "Key Roles: AAW taps into Dryden's knowledge, experience and flight research savvy." *The X-Press*, Special Active Aeroelastic Wing Edition (December 17, 2003).

Levine, Jay. "Phase Two: Effectiveness of wing twist for roll control will be explored." *The X-Press*: Special Active Aeroelastic Wing Edition (December 17, 2003).

Levine, Jay, and Sarah Merlin. "Phase One: First flights set the stage for advances in AAW technology." *The X-Press*: Special Active Aeroelastic Wing Edition (December 17, 2003.

Lockheed Martin. "LMTAS Statement of Work for F-16 Active Aeroelastic Wing Flight Demonstration Program." Lockheed Martin Tactical Aircraft Systems, Fort Worth, TX, provided by Dave Voracek, NASA Dryden Flight Research Center, from personal files (1995).

McKay, M.J. Memo re: "Active Flexible Wing Technology Flight Test Demonstration Proposal 94-1028." Rockwell International, North American Aircraft Division (February 25, 1994).

NASA. "Back to the Future: Active Aeroelastic Wing Flight Research." NASA Fact Sheet, *http://www.nasa.gov/centers/dryden/news/FactSheets/FS-061-DFRC.html*, December 2009.

NASA. Notes on "Active Aeroelastic Wing (AAW) Technology Previous Efforts/Opportunities." Provided by Dave Voracek, NASA Dryden Flight Research Center, from personal files (March 1996).

NASA. Ewers, Richard G., research pilot biography, NASA Dryden Flight Research Center, *http://www.nasa.gov/centers/dryden/news/Biographies/Pilots/bd-dfrc-p025.html*, February 2012.

NASA. Purifoy, Dana D., research pilot biography, NASA Dryden Flight Research Center, *http://www.nasa.gov/centers/dryden/news/Biographies/Pilots/bd-dfrc-p013.html*, September 2010.

Rivas, Mauricio. "Active Aeroelastic Wing Project Dryden Independent Review, Flight Operations Engineering." Briefing to AAW Flight Readiness Review Board, provided by Dave Voracek, NASA Dryden Flight Research Center, from personal files (March 2002).

Szalai, Kenneth J., George K. Richey, and James P. Brady. "DRAFT— Active Aeroelastic Wing (AAW) Program Annex to the Memorandum of Understanding Between USAF Wright Laboratory (WL), Air Force Flight Test Center (AFFTC), and NASA Dryden Flight Research Center (DFRC)." January 1996.

Acknowledgments

The author would like to thank the many people who helped make this book possible. First of all, thanks to Tony Springer, NASA Aeronautics Research Mission Directorate, for sponsoring this project. I am grateful for the efforts of many people at NASA Dryden Flight Research Center including, but not limited to, Leslie Williams, Carla Thomas, Dick Ewers, and Karl Bender. Thanks to Chris Yates, Ben Weinstein, and Kurt von Tish at Media Fusion for preparing the manuscript for publication. Special thanks to David Voracek, Ed Pendleton, Al Bowers, Ken Griffin, Pete Flick, and Bill Lokos—who reviewed the material for technical accuracy—and, especially, to Sarah Merlin for copy-editing the final manuscript.

About the Author

Peter W. Merlin is an aerospace historian under contract to the NASA Aeronautics Research Mission Directorate. Working at Dryden Flight Research Center since 1997, he has authored a variety of books, including several NASA Special Publications on aeronautical research projects, as well as two volumes on aerospace safety. He served as coauthor of research pilot Donald Mallick's autobiography, *The Smell of Kerosene: A Test Pilot's Odyssey*; and *X-Plane Crashes—Exploring Experimental, Rocket Plane and Spycraft Incidents, Accidents and Crash Sites*, with Tony Moore. He has also written several technical papers for the American Institute of Aeronautics and Astronautics as well as numerous journal articles on aerospace history and technology. In addition, he serves as contributing editor for historical publications at Dryden and has appeared in more than a dozen documentary television programs for Discovery Channel, History Channel, National Geographic Channel, and others. He holds a bachelor of science degree in aviation management from Embry-Riddle Aeronautical University.

Index

Numbers in **bold** indicate pages with illustrations and figures.

I

J

K

L

M